Contents

Our parents had gone out, and were walking slowly under the chestnut trees in the garden, and had left us entirely alone for a few minutes. I went up to her and took both her hands into mine, which were trembling, and gently drawing her close to me, I whispered:

"How happy I am, Elaine, and how I love you!" and I kissed her almost timidly, on the dimple. She trembled, as if from the pain of a burn, blushed deeply, and with an affectionate look she said: "I love you also, Jacques, and I am very happy!"

That embarrassment, that sudden emotion which revealed the perfect spotlessness of a pure mind, the instinctive recoil of virginity, that childlike innocence, that blush of modesty, delighted me above everything as a presage of happiness. It seemed to me as if I were unworthy of her; I was almost ashamed of bringing to her and of putting into her small, saintlike hands the remains of a damaged heart, that had been polluted by debauchery, that miserable thing which had served as a toy for unworthy mistresses, which was intoxicated with lies, and felt as if it would die of bitterness and disgust.

PART II

How quickly she has become accustomed to me, how suddenly she has turned into a woman and become metamorphosed! Already she no longer is at all like the artless girl, the sensitive child, to whom I did not know what to say, and whose sudden questions disconcerted me.

She is coquettish, and there is seduction in her attitudes, in her gestures, in her laugh, and in her

Mad

PART I

FOR days and days, nights and nights, I had dreamed of that first kiss which was to consecrate our engagement, and I knew not on what spot I should put my lips. Not on her forehead, that was accustomed to family caresses, nor on her light hair, which mercenary hands had dressed, nor on her eyes, whose curling lashes looked like little wings, because that would have made me think of the farewell caress which closes the eyelids of some dead woman whom one has adored, nor her lovely mouth, which I will not, which I must not, possess until that divine moment when Elaine will at last belong to me altogether and for always, but on that delicious little dimple which comes in one of her cheeks when she is happy, when she smiles, and which excited me as much as her voice did with languorous softness, on that evening when our flirtation began, at the Souverettes'.

touch. One might think that she was trying her power over me, and that she guesses that I no longer have any will of my own. She does with me whatever she likes, and I am quite incapable of resisting the beautiful charm that emanates from her, and I feel carried away by her caressing hands, and so happy that I am at times frightened at the excess of my own felicity.

My life now passes amid the most delicious of punishments, those afternoons and evenings that we spend together, those unconstrained moments when, sitting on the sofa together, she rests her head on my shoulder, holds my hands, and half shuts her beautiful eyes while we settle what our future life shall be; when I cover her with kisses and inhale the odor of all that soft fluffy hair that is as fine as silk, like a halo round her imperial brow. All this excites me, unsettles me, kills me, and yet I feel inclined to shed tears when the time comes for us to part, and I really only exist when I am with Elaine.

I can scarcely sleep; I see her rise up in the darkness, delicate, fair, and pink, so supple, so elegant with her small waist and tiny hands and feet, her graceful head and that look of mockery and of coaxing which lies in her smile, that brightness of the dawn which illuminates her looks, and when I think that she is going to become my wife, I feel inclined to sing, and to shout out my amorous folly into the silence of the night.

Elaine also seems to be at the end of her strength, has grown languid and nervous; she would like to wipe out the fortnight that we still have to wait, and so little does she hide her longing that one of her uncles, Colonel d'Orthez, said after dinner the other evening: "By Jove, my children, one would take you for two soldiers who are looking forward to their furlough!"

PART III

I do not know what I felt, or whence those fears came which so suddenly assailed me, and took possession of my whole being, like a flight of poisoned arrows. The nearer the day approaches that I am so ardently longing for, on which Elaine will take my name and belong to me, the more anxious, nervous, and tormented by the uncertainty of the morrow I feel.

I love and I am passionately loved, and few couples start on the unknown journey of a totally new life and enter into matrimony with such hopes, and the same assurance of happiness, as we two.

I have such faith in the girl I am going to marry, and have made her such vows of love, that I should certainly kill myself without a moment's hesitation if anything were to happen to separate us, to force us to a *comme il faut* but irremediable rupture, or if Elaine were seized by some illness which carried her off quickly. And yet I hesitate, I am afraid, for I know that many others have made shipwreck, lost their love on the way, disenchanted their wives, and have themselves been disenchanted in those first essays of possession.

What does Elaine expect in her vague innocence, which has been lessened by the half-confidences of married friends, by semi-avowals, by all the kisses of this sort of apprenticeship which is a court of love? What does she possess? What does she hope for? Oh! to think that one is risking one's whole future happiness at such a hazardous game, that the merest trifle might make a woman completely ridiculous or hopeful, and make an idolized woman laugh or cry!

I do not know a more desirable, prettier, or more attractive being in the whole world than Elaine; I am worn out by feverish love, and I wish every particle of her being to belong to me; I love her ardently, but I would willingly give half that I possess to have got through this ordeal, to be a week older, *and still happy!*

PART IV

My mother-in-law took me aside yesterday, while they were dancing, and with tears in her eyes she said in a tremulous voice:

"You are going to possess the most precious object that we possess here, and what we love best—I beg you to always spare the slightest unhappiness, and to be kind and gentle toward her. I count on your uprightness and affection to guide her and protect her in this dangerous life in Paris." And then, giving way to her feelings more and more, she added: "I do not think that you suppose that I have tried to instruct her in her new duties or to disturb her charming innocence, which has been my work; when two persons worship each other as you two do, a girl learns what she is ignorant of so quickly and so well!"

I very nearly burst out laughing in her face, for such a theatrical phrase appeared to me both ridiculous and doubtful. So that respectable woman had always been a passive, pliable, inert object, who never had one moment of vibration, of tender emotion in her husband's arms, and I understood why, as I wasted time at the clubs, he escaped from her as soon as possible and formed other liaisons which cost him dear, but in which he found at least some appearance of love.

And that piece of advice, at the last moment, which was so commonplace and natural, and which I ought to have expected, enervated me and, in spite of myself, plunged me into a state of perplexity, from which I could not extricate myself. I remembered those absurd stories which we hear among friends, after a good dinner. What would be that last trial of our love for her and for me, and would that love which then was my whole life come out of the ordeal lessened or increased tenfold? And when I looked at the couch on which Elaine, my adored Elaine, was sitting, with her head half-hidden behind the feathers of her fan, she whispered in a rather vexed voice:

"How cross you look, my dear Jacques! Is the fact that you are to be married the cause of it? And you have such a mocking look on your face. If the thought of it terrifies you too much, there is still time to say *no!*"

And, delighted, bewitched by her caressing looks, I said in a low voice, almost into her small ear:

"I adore you; and these last moments that still separate us seem centuries to me, my dear Elaine!"

PART V

There were tiresome ceremonies yesterday and to-day, which I went through almost mechanically.

First, there is the *yes* before the mayor at the civil ceremony, like some everyday response in church, which one is in a hurry to get over, and which has almost the suggestion of an imperious law, to which one is bound to submit, and of a state of bondage, which will, perhaps, be very irksome, since the whole of existence is made up of chance.

And then the service in church, with the decorated altar, the voices of the choir, the solemn music of the organ, the unctuous address of the old priest, who marked his periods, who seemed quite proud of having prepared Elaine for confirmation, and then the procession of the vestry, the shaking hands, and the greetings of people whom you scarcely see, and whom you do, or do not, recognize.

Under the long tulle veil, which almost covered her, with the symbolical orange flowers on her bright, light hair, in her white dress, with her downcast eyes and her graceful figure, Elaine looked to me like a Psyche, whose innocent heart was vowed to love. I felt how vain and artificial all this form was, how little this show counted before the kiss, the triumphant, revealing, maddening kiss, which sealed our nuptial vow.

PART VI

Elaine loves me as much as I adore her.

She left her parental abode, as if she were going to some festivity, without once turning toward all that she had left behind, in the way of affection and recollection, and without even a farewell tear.

She looked like a bird which had escaped from its cage and does not know where to settle, which beats its wings in the intoxication of the light, and which warbles incessantly. She repeated the same words, as if she were dazed, and her laugh sounded like the cooing of a pigeon, and looking into my eyes, with her eyes full of languor and her arms round my neck like a bracelet and with her burning cheek against mine, she suddenly exclaimed:

"I say, my darling, would you not give ten years of your life to have already got to the end of the journey?"

This question so disconcerted me that I did not know what to reply, and my brain reeled, as if I had been at the edge of a precipice. Did she already know what her mother had not told her? Had she already learned what she ought to have been ignorant of? And had that heart, which I used to compare to the Vessel of Election, of which the litanies of Our Lady speak, already been damaged?

Oh! white veils that hide the blushes, the half-closed eyes, and the trembling lips of some Psyche; oh! little hands which you raised in an attitude of prayer toward the lighted and decorated altar; oh! innocent and charming questions, which delighted me to the depths of my being, and which seemed to me to be an absolute promise of happiness, were you nothing but a lie, and a wonderfully well-acted piece of trickery?

But was I not wrong, and an idiot, to allow such thoughts to take possession of me and to poison my deep, absorbing love, which was now my only law and my only object, by odious and foolish suggestions? What an abject and miserable nature I must have, for such a simple, affectionate, natural question to disturb me so, when I ought immediately to have replied to Elaine's question, with all my heart that belonged to her:

"Yes, ten or twenty years, because you are my happiness, my desire, my love!"

PART VII

Elaine was still sleeping when I arose, and I did not choose to wait until she woke up. Her complexion was almost transparent, her lips were half-open, as if she were dreaming, and she seemed so overcome with sleep that I felt much emotion when I looked at her.

I drank four glasses of champagne, one after the other, as quickly as I could, but it did not quench my thirst. I was feverish, and would have given anything in the world for something to interest me suddenly and have absorbed me and lifted me out of that slough in which my heart and my brain were being engulfed, as if in a quicksand. I did not venture to avow to myself what was making me mad with grief, or to scrutinize the muddy bottom of my present thoughts sincerely and courageously, to question myself and to pull myself together.

It would have been so odious, so infamous, to harbor such suspicions unjustly, to accuse that adorable creature who was not yet twenty, whom I loved, and *who seemed to love me,* without having certain proofs, that I felt that I was blushing at the idea that I had any doubt of her innocence. Ah! Why did I marry?

I had a sufficient income to enable me to live as I liked, to play the gallant to beautiful women who pleased me, whom I chanced to meet and who amused me, and who sometimes gave me unexpected proofs of affection, but I had never allowed myself to be caught altogether, and in order to keep my heart warm I had some romantic and sentimental friendships with women in society, some of those delightful flirtations which have an appearance of love, which fill up the idleness of a useless life with a number of unexpected sensations, with small duties and vague, subtle pleasures!

And was I now going to be like one of those ships which an unskilful turn of the helm runs ashore as it is leaving the harbor? What terrible trials were awaiting me, what sorrows and what struggles?

A humorous friend said to me one night in joke at the club, when I had just broken one of those banks which form an epoch in a player's life:

"If I were in your place, Jacques, I should distrust such runs of luck as that, for one always has to pay for them sooner or later!"

Sooner or later!

I half opened the bedroom door gently. Elaine was in one of those heavy sleeps similar to those that follow intoxication. Who could tell whether, when she opened her eyes and called me, surprised at not finding me, her whole being would not become languid, and suddenly sink into a state of prostration? I wanted to reason with myself, and bring myself face to face with those cursed suggestions, as one does with a skittish horse before some object that frightens it, and to evoke the recollection of every hour, every minute, of that first night, and to extract the secret from her.

Elaine's looks and radiant smile were overflowing with happiness, and she had the air of a conqueror who is proud of his triumph, for she was now a woman, and we had at least been alone in this modernized country house, which had been redecorated and smartened up to serve as the frame for our affection! She hardly seemed to know what she was saying or doing, and ran from room to room in her light *negligée* dress of mauve crape, without exactly knowing where to sit, and almost dazzled by the light of the lamps that had large shades to represent rose leaves over them.

There was no embarrassment, no hesitation, no shamefaced looks, no recoiling from the arms that were stretched out to her; none of those delightful little pieces of awkwardness which show a virgin soul free from all perversion, in her manner of sitting on my knees, of putting her bare arms round my neck. She laughed nervously, and her supple form trembled when I kissed her, and she said things to me that were only suitable for being whispered, while a strange languor overshadowed her eyes and dilated her nostrils.

And suddenly, with a mocking gesture which seemed to bid defiance to the repast that was laid on a small table, cold meat of various kinds, plates of fruit and of cakes, the ice pail, from which the neck of a bottle of champagne protruded, she said:

" I am not at all hungry, dear; let us not eat until later; what do you say? "

She half turned round to the large bed, which looked white in the shadow of the recess in which it stood, with its two white, untouched, almost solemn pillows. She was not smiling any more; there was a bluish gleam in her eyes, like that of burning alcohol, and I lost my head. Elaine did not try to escape, and did not utter a complaint.

Oh! that night of torture and delight, that night which ought never to have ended!

I determined that I would be as patient as a policeman who is trying to discover the traces of a crime, that I would investigate the past of this girl, about which I knew nothing, as I should be sure to discover some proof, some important reminiscence, some servant who had been her accomplice.

And yet I adored her, my pretty, my divine Elaine, and I would consent no matter to what if only she were what I dreamed her, what I wished her to be, if only this nightmare would go and no longer rise up between her and me.

When she woke up she spoke to me in her coaxing voice. Oh! her kisses, again her kisses, always her kisses, in spite of everything!

Oh! to have believed blindly, to have believed on my knees that she was not lying, that she was not making a mockery of my tenderness, and that she had never belonged, and never would belong, to any one but me!

PART VIII

I wished that I could have transformed myself into one of those crafty, unctuous priests to whom women confess their most secret faults, to whom they intrust their souls and frequently ask for advice, and that Elaine would have come and knelt at the grating of the confessional, where I should press her closely with questions, and gradually extract sincere confidences from her.

Nowadays, as soon as I am by the side of a young

or old married woman I try to give our conversation a knowing turn; I forget all reserve, and I try to make her talk on the only subject that interests and holds me, to extract from her, if possible, a recital of her true heart feelings. Was she shy or bold in the presence of her husband on those first days of their married life? Some do not appear to understand me, blush, leave me as if I were some unpleasant, ill-mannered person and had offended them; as if I had tried to force open the precious casket in which they keep their sweetest recollections.

Others understand me only too well, scent something equivocal and ridiculous, though they do not exactly know what, make me go on, and finally get out of the difficulty by some subtle piece of impertinence and a burst of teasing laughter.

Two or three at most, and they were those pretty little upstarts who talk at random and brag about their vice, and whom one could soon not leave a leg to stand upon, were one to take the trouble, have related their impressions to me with ironical complaisance, and I found nothing in what they told me that reassured me, nor could I discover anything serious, true, or moving in it.

That supreme initiation amused them as much as if it had been a scene from a comedy; the small amount of affection that they felt for the man with whom their existence had been welded grew less and evaporated altogether—and they remembered nothing about it except its ridiculous and hateful side, and described it as a sort of pantomime in which they played a bad part. But these did not love and were not adored as Elaine was. They married either from interest, or that they might not remain old maids, that they might have more liberty and escape from troublesome guardianship.

Foolish dolls, without either heart or head, they had neither that almost diseased nervosity, nor that requirement for affection, nor that instinct of love which I discovered in my wife's nature, and which attracted me at the same time that it terrified me.

Besides, who could convince me of my errors? Who could dissipate that darkness in which I was lost? What miracle could restore *all* my belief in her again?

PART IX

Elaine felt that I was hiding something from her, that I was unhappy, that, as it were, some threatening obstacle had risen up between her and me, that some insupportable suspicion was oppressing me, torturing me and keeping me from her arms, was poisoning and disturbing that affection in which I had hoped to find fresh youth, absolute happiness, my dream of dreams.

She never spoke to me about it, however, but seemed to recoil from a definite explanation which might make shipwreck of her love. She surrounded me with endearing attentions, and appeared to be trying to make my life so pleasant to me that nothing in the world could draw me from it. And she would certainly cure me, if this madness of mine were not, alas! like those wounds which are constantly reopening, and which no balm can heal.

But at times I lived again, I imagined that her caresses had exorcised me, that I was saved, that doubt was no longer gnawing at my heart, that I was going to adore her again as I used to. I would throw myself at her knees and put my lips on her little hands, which she abandoned to me; I looked at her lovely, limpid eyes as if they had been a piece of a blue sky that appeared amid black storm clouds, and I whispered, with something like a sob in my throat:

"You love me, do you not, with all your heart, you love me as much as I love you; tell me so again, my dear love; tell me that, and nothing but that!"

And she used to reply eagerly, with a smile of joy on her lips:

"Do you not know it? Do you not see every moment that I love you, that you have taken entire possession of me, and that I only live for you and by you?"

And her kisses gave me new life, and intoxicated me, as when one returns from a long journey and had been in peril, and despairs of ever seeing some beloved object again, and one meets with a sort of frenzied embrace, and forgets everything in that divine feeling that one is going to die of happiness.

PART X

But these were only ephemeral clear spots in our sky, and the crises which accompanied them only grew more bitter and terrible. I knew that Elaine was growing more and more uneasy at the apparent strangeness of my character, that she suffered from it, and that it affected her nerves, that the existence to which I was condemning her in spite of myself, that all this immoderate love of mine, followed by fits of inexplicable coldness and melancholy, disconcerted her, so that she was no longer the same, and kept away from me. She could not hide her grief, and was continually worrying me with questions of affectionate pity. She repeated the same things over and over again, with hateful persistence. She had vexed me, without knowing it? Was I already tired of my married life, and did I regret my lost liberty? Had I any private troubles which I had not told her of; heavy debts which I did not know how to pay? Was it family matters or some former connection with a woman that I had broken off suddenly, and that now threatened to create a scandal? Was I being worried by anonymous letters? What was it, in a word? What was it?

My denials only exasperated her, so that she sulked in silence, while her brain worked and her heart grew hard toward me; but could I, as a matter of fact, tell her of my suspicions which were filling my life with gloom and annihilating me? Would it not be odious and vile to accuse her of such a fall, without any proofs or any clue, and would she ever forget such an insult?

I almost envied those unfortunate wretches who had the right to be jealous, who had to fight against a woman's coquettish and light behavior, and who had to defend their honor that was threatened by some poacher on the preserves of love. They had a target to aim at; they knew their enemies and knew what they were doing, while I was wandering in a land of terrible mirages, was struggling in the midst of vague suppositions, and was causing my own troubles, and was enraged with her past, which was, I felt sure, as white and pure as any bridal veil.

Ah! It would be better to blow my brains out, I thought to myself, than to prolong such a situation! I had had enough of it. I scarcely lived, and I wished to know all that Elaine had done before we became engaged. I wanted to know whether I was the first or the second, and I determined to know it, even if I had to sacrifice years of my life in inquiry, and to lower myself to compromising words and acts, and to every species of artifice, and to spend everything that I possessed!

She might believe whatever she liked, for after all I should only laugh at it. We might have been so happy, and there were so many who envied me, and who would gladly have consented to take my place!

PART XI

I no longer knew where I was going, but was like a train moving at full speed through a dense fog, and which in vain disturbs the perfect silence of the sleeping country with its puffing and shrill whistles; when the driver cannot distinguish the changing lights of the disks nor the signals, and when soon some terrible crash will send the train off the rails, and the carriages will become a heap of ruins.

I was afraid of going mad, and at times I asked myself whether any of my family had shown any signs of mental aberration and had been locked up in a lunatic asylum, and whether the life of constant fast pleasure, of turning night into day, and of frequent violent emotions, that I had led for years, had not at last affected my brain. If I had believed in anything, and in the science of the occult, which haunts so many restless brains, I should have imagined that some enemy was bewitching me and laying invisible snares for me, that he was suggesting those actions which were quite unworthy of the frank, upright, and well-bred man that I was, and was trying to destroy the happiness of which she and I had dreamed.

For a whole week I devoted myself to that hateful business of playing the spy, and to those inquiries which were killing me. I had succeeded in discovering the lady's maid who had been in Elaine's service before we were married, and whom she loved as if she had been her foster sister, who used to accompany her whenever she went out, when she went to visit the poor and when she went for a walk, who used to wake her every morning, do her hair, and dress her. She was young and rather pretty, and one saw that Paris had improved her and given her a polish, and that she knew her difficult business from end to end.

I had found out, however, that her virtue was only apparent, especially since she had changed employers; that she was fond of going to the public balls, and that she divided her favors between a man who came from her part of the country and who was a sergeant in a dragoon regiment, and a footman, and that she spent all her money on horse races and on dress. I felt sure that I should be able to make her talk and get the truth out of her, either by money or cunning, and so I asked her to meet me early one morning in a quiet square.

She listened to me first of all in astonishment,

without replying yes or no, as if she did not understand what I was aiming at, or with what object I was asking her all these questions about her former mistress; but when I offered her a few hundred francs to loosen her tongue, as I was impatient to get the matter over and pretended to know that she had managed interviews for Elaine with her lovers, that they were known and followed, that she was in the habit of frequenting quiet bachelors' quarters, from which she returned late, the sly little wench frowned angrily, shrugged her shoulders, and exclaimed:

"What pigs some men are to have such ideas, and cause such an excellent person as Mademoiselle Elaine any unhappiness! Look here, you disgust me with your banknotes and your dirty stories, and I don't choose to say what you ought to wear on your head!"

She turned her back on me and hurried off, and her insolence, that indignant reply which she had given me, rejoiced me to the depths of my heart, like soothing balm that lulls the pain.

I should have liked to call her back to me and tell her that it was all a joke, that I was devotedly in love with my wife, that I was always on the watch to hear her praised, but she was already out of sight, and I felt that I was ridiculous and mean, that I had lowered myself by what I had done; and I swore that I would profit by such a humiliating lesson, and for the future show myself to Elaine as the trusting and ardent husband that she deserved; and I thought myself cured, altogether cured.

And yet I was again a prey to the same bad thoughts, to the same doubts, and persuaded that that girl had lied to me just as all women lie when they are on the defensive, that she made fun of me, that perhaps *some one* had foreseen this scene and had told her what to say and made sure of her silence, just as her complicity had been gained. Thus I shall always knock up against some barrier, and struggle in this wretched darkness and this mire from which I cannot extricate myself!

PART XII

Nobody knew anything. Neither the Superior of the convent where she had been brought up until she was sixteen, nor the servants who had waited on her, nor the governesses who had finished her education, could remember that Elaine had been difficult to check or to teach, or that she had had any other ideas than those of her age. She had certainly shown no precocious coquetry and disquieting instincts at school that would begin the inevitable eclogue of Daphnis and Chloe over again.

However—oh! I felt it too much for it to be nothing but a chimera and a mirage—it was no pure girl who threw her arms round my neck so lovingly, and who returned my first kisses so deliciously, who was attracted by my society, who gave no signs of surprise and uttered no complaint, who appeared to forget everything when in my society. No, no, a thousand times no, that could not have been a pure woman.

I ought to have cast off that intoxication which was bewitching me, and to have rushed out of the room where such a lie was being consummated; I ought to have profited by her moments of amiable weakness, while she was incapable of collecting her thoughts, when she would with tears have confessed an old fault, for which the unhappy girl had not, perhaps, been altogether responsible. Perhaps by my entreaties, or even perhaps by violence, in terror at my furious looks, when my features would have been distorted by rage and my hands clinched in spite of myself in a gesture of menace and of murder, I might have forced her to open her heart, to show me its defilement, and to tell me its sad love episode.

How do I know whether her disconsolateness might not have moved me to pity, whether I should not have wept with her at the heavy cross that we both of us had to bear, whether I should not have forgiven her and opened my arms wide, so that she might have thrown herself into them as into a peaceful refuge?

Who could tell me or come to my aid? Who could give me the proofs, the real, undeniable proofs, either that I was an infamous wretch to suspect Elaine, whom I ought to have worshiped with my eyes shut, or that she was guilty, that she had lied, and that I had the right to cast her out of my life and to treat her like a worthless woman?

PART XIII

If I had married when I was quite young, before I had wallowed in the mire of Paris, from which one can never afterward free one's self, for heart and body both retain indelible marks of it, if experiences had not disgusted me with belief in any woman, if I had not been weaned from supreme illusions and surfeited with everything to the marrow, should I have these abominable ideas?

I waited almost until I was beginning to decline in life before I took the right path and sought refuge in port, before going to what is pure and virtuous, and before listening to the continual advice of those who love me. I passed too suddenly from those lies, from those ephemeral enjoyments, from that satiety which depraves us, from vice in which one tries to acquire renewed strength and vigor and to discover some new and unknown sensation, to the pure sentimentalities of an engagement, to the unspeakable delights of a life that was common to two, to that first communion which ought to constitute married life.

If, instead of becoming involved in an engagement and forming a resolution so quickly—I had been afraid that somebody else would be beforehand with me and rob me of Elaine's heart, or that I should relapse into my former habits—if, instead of lacking moral strength and character enough, in case I might have had to wait; if I had backed out without entering into any engagement and without having bound my life to that of the adorable girl whom chance had thrown in my way, it would surely have been far better. If I had waited, prepared myself, questioned myself, and accustomed myself to that metamorphosis; if I had purified myself and forgotten the past, as in those retreats which precede the solemn ceremony when pious souls pronounce their indissoluble vows, how much wiser I should have been!

The reaction had been too sudden and violent for such a convalescent as I was. I worked myself up, and pictured to myself something so white, so virginal, so paradisiacal, such complete ignorance, such unconquerable modesty, and such delicious awkwardness, that Elaine's gayety, her unconstraint, her fearlessness, and her kisses bewildered me, roused my suspicions, and filled me with anguish.

And yet I know how all, or nearly all, girls are educated in these days, and that the ignorant, simple ones only exist in the drama, and I know also that they hear and learn too many things, both at home and in society, not to have the intuition of the results of love.

Elaine loves me with all her heart, for she has told me so time after time, and she repeats it to me more ardently than ever when I take her into my arms and appear happy. She must have seen that her beauty had, in a manner, converted me; that in order to possess her I had renounced many seductions and a long life of enjoyment; and perhaps she would no longer please me if she were too much of the little girl, and would appear ridiculous to me if she showed her fears by any entreaty, or gesture, or any sigh.

As the people in the South say, she would have acted the brave woman, and boasted, so that no complaint might betray her, and have imparted the wild tenderness of a jealous heart to her kisses, and have attempted a struggle, which would certainly have been useless, against those recollections of mine, with which she thought I must be filled, in spite of myself.

I accused myself so that I might no longer accuse her. I studied my malady; I knew quite well I was wrong, and I wished to be wrong. I measured the stupidity and the disgrace of such suspicions, and, nevertheless, in spite of everything, they assailed me again, watched me traitorously, and I was carried away and devoured by them.

Ah! Was there in the whole world, even among the most wretched beggars that were dying of starvation, whom nature squeezes in a vise, as it were, or among the victims of love, anybody who could say that he was more wretched than I?

PART XIV

This morning Comte de Saulnac, who was lunching here, told us a terrible story of a physician who had drugged or hypnotized a farmer's young daughter, who had been sent to him as a patient, and how he had brutally assaulted her.

Before he had finished I noticed an evil look on Elaine's face such as I had never before seen, and with vibrating nostrils she exclaimed in a hard voice:

" To think that such a monster was not sent to the guillotine! " But unless Elaine was a monster of wickedness, unless she had no heart and knew how to lie and to deceive as well as a girl whose only pleasure consists in making all those who are captivated by her beauty play the laughable part of dupes, unless that mask of youth concealed a most polluted soul, if there had been any unhappy episode in her life, would not something visible, something disgusting, attacks of low spirits and of gloom and disgust with everything, have remained, which would have shown the progress of some mysterious malady, the gradual weakening of the brain, and the enlargement of an incurable wound?

She would have cried occasionally, would have

been lost in thought and become confused when spoken to; she would scarcely have taken any interest in anything that happened, either at home or elsewhere. Kisses would have become a torture to her, and would have only excited a fever of revolt in her inanimate being.

I fancy that I can see such a victim of inexorable Destiny, as if she were a consumptive woman whose days are numbered, and who knows it. She smiles feebly when any one tries to get her out of her torpor, to amuse her, and to instill a little hope into her soul. She does not speak, but remains sitting silently at a window for whole days together, and one might think that her large, dreamy eyes are looking at strange sights in the depths of the sky, and see a long, attractive road there. But Elaine, on the contrary, thought of nothing but of amusing herself, of enjoying life and of laughing, and added all the tricks of a girl who has just left school to her seductive grace of a young woman. She carried men away with her; she was most seductive, and loving seemed to be her creation. She thought of nothing but of little coquettish acts that made her more adorable, and of tender innuendoes that triumph over everything, that bring men to their knees and tempt them.

It was thus that I formerly dreamed of the woman who was to be my wife, and this was the manner in which I looked on life in common; and now this perpetual joy irritates me like a challenge, like some piece of insolent boasting, and those lips that seek mine and which offer themselves so alluringly and coaxingly to me make me sad and torture me, as if they breathed nothing but a lie.

Ah! If she had been the lover of another man

before marriage, if she had belonged to some one else besides me, it could only have been from love, without altogether knowing what she wanted or what she was doing! And now, because she had acquired a name by marriage, because she had accidentaly extricated herself from that false step and thought she had won the game, now she fancied that I had not perceived anything, that I adored her and possessed her absolutely.

How wretched I was! Should I never be able to escape from that night which was growing darker and darker, which was imprisoning me, driving me mad, and raising an increasing and impenetrable barrier between Elaine and me? Would not she, in the end, be the stronger, she whom I loved so dearly, would not she envelop me in so much love that at last I should again find the happiness that I had lost, as if it were a calm, sunlit haven, and thus forget this horrible nightmare when I fell on my knees before her beauty, with a contrite heart and pricked by remorse, and happy to give myself to her forever, altogether and more passionately than at the divine period of our betrothal?

PART XV

Even the sight of our bedroom became painful to me. I was afraid of it; I was uncomfortable there, and felt a kind of repulsion in going there. It seemed to me as if Elaine were repeating a part that some one else had taught her, and I almost hoped that in a moment of forgetfulness she would allow her secret to escape her, and pronounce some name that was not mine, and I used to keep awake, with my ears on the alert, in the hope that she might betray herself in her sleep and murmur some revealing word, as she recalled the past, and my temples throbbed and my whole body trembled with excitement.

But when this was over and I saw her sleeping peacefully as a little girl who was tired with playing, with parted lips and disheveled hair, and measured the full extent of the stupidity of my hatred and the sacrilegious madness of my jealousy, my heart softened and I fell into such a state of profound and absolute distress that I thought I should have died of it, and large drops of cold perspiration ran down my cheeks and tears fell from my eyes, and I got up, so that my sobs might not disturb her rest and wake her.

As this could not continue, however, I told her one day that I felt so exhausted and ill that I should prefer to sleep in my own room. She appeared to believe me, and merely said:

"As you please, my dear!" but her blue eyes suddenly assumed such an anxious, such a grieved look that I turned my head aside, so as not to see them.

PART XVI

I was again in the old house, *and without her,* in the old house where Elaine used to spend all her holidays, in the room whose shutters had not been opened since our departure seven months ago.

Why did I go there, where the calm of the country, the silence of the solitude, and my recollections irritated me and recalled my trouble, where I suffered even more than I did in Paris, and where I thought of Elaine every moment I seemed to see her and to hear her, in a species of hallucination?

What did her letters that I had taken out of her writing table, which she had used as a girl; what did her ball cards, which were stuck round her looking-glass, in which she used to admire herself formerly; what did her dresses, her dressing-gowns, and the dusty furniture whose repose my trembling hands violated, tell me? Nothing, and always nothing!

At table I used to speak with the worthy couple who had never left the mansion and who appeared to look upon themselves as its second masters, with the apparent good nature of a man who was in love with his wife and who wished only to speak about her, who took an interest in the smallest detail of her childhood and youth, with all the jovial familiarity which encourages peasants to talk, and when a few glasses of white wine had loosened their tongues they would talk about her whom they loved as if she had been their child, and at other times I used to question the farmers, when they came to settle their accounts.

Had Elaine the bridle on her neck as so many girls had? Did she like the country? Were the peasants fond of her, and did she show any preference for one or the other? Were many people invited for the shooting, and did she visit much with the other ladies in the neighborhood?

And they drank with their elbows resting on the table in front of me, uttered her praises in a voice as monotonous as a spinning wheel, lost themselves in endless, senseless chatter which made me yawn in spite of myself, and told me her girlish tricks, which certainly did not disclose what was haunting me, the traces of that first love, that perilous flirtation, that foolish escapade which Elaine might have experienced.

Old and young men and women spoke of her with something like devotion, and all said how kind and charitable she was, and as merry as a bird on a bright day; they said she pitied their wretchedness and their troubles, and was still the young girl in spite of her long dresses, and fearing nothing, while even the animals loved her.

She was almost always alone, and was never troubled with any companions; she seemed to shun the house, hide herself in the park when the bell announced some unexpected visit, and when one of her aunts, Madame de Pleissac, said to her:

"Do you think that you will ever find a husband with your stand-offish manners?" she replied, with a burst of laughter:

"Oh! Very well, then, auntie, I shall do without one!"

She had never given a handle to spiteful chatter or to slander, and had not flirted with the best-looking young man in the neighborhood, any more than she had with the officers who stayed at the château during the maneuvers, or the neighbors who came to see her parents. And some of them even, old men whom years of work had bent like vine stocks and had tanned like the leather bottles which are used by caravans in the East, used to say, with tears in their dim eyes:

"Ah! When you married our young lady we all said that there would not be a happier man in the whole world than you!"

Ought I to have believed them? Were they not simple, frank souls, ignorant of wiles and of lies, who had no interest in deceiving me, who had lived near Elaine while she was growing up and becoming a woman, and who had been familiar with her?

Could I be the only one who doubted Elaine, the only one who accused her and suspected her, I who loved her so madly, I whose only hope, only desire, only happiness she was? May Heaven guide me on this bad road on which I have lost my way, where I am calling for help and where my misery is increasing every day, and grant me the infinite pleasure of being able to enjoy her caresses without any ill feeling, and to be able to love her as she loves me. And if I must expiate my old faults, and this infamous doubt which I am ashamed of not being immediately able to cast from me, if I must pay for my unmerited happiness with usury, I hope that I may be given to death as a prey, only provided that I might belong to her, idolize her, believe in her kisses, believe in her beauty and in her love, for one hour, for even a few moments!

PART XVII

To-day I suddenly remembered a strange evening which I spent when I was a bachelor at Madame d'Ecoussens', where all of us, some with secret and insurmountable agony and others with absolute indifference, went into one of the small rooms where a female professor of palmistry, who was then in vogue and whose name I have forgotten, had installed herself.

When it came to my turn to sit opposite to her,

as if I had been going to make my confession, she took my hands into her long, slender fingers, felt them, squeezed them, and triturated them, as if they had been a lump of wax which she was about to model into shape.

Severely dressed in black, with a pensive face, thin lips, and almost copper-colored eyes, and neither young nor old, this woman had something commanding, imperious, disturbing about her, and I must confess that my heart beat more violently than usual while she looked at the lines in my left hand through a strong magnifying glass, where the mysterious characters of some Satanic conjuring look appear and form a capital M.

She was very interesting, occasionally discovered fragments of my past and gave mysterious hints, as if her looks were following the strange roads of Destiny in those unequal, confused curves. She told me in brief words that I should have and had had some opportunities, that I was wasting my physical, more than my moral, strength in all kinds of love affairs that did not last long, and that the day when I really loved, or when, to use her expression, I was fairly caught, would be to me the prelude of intense sufferings, a real way of the Cross and of an illness of which I should never be cured. Then, as she examined my line of life, that which surrounds the thick part of the thumb, the lady in black suddenly grew gloomy, frowned, and appeared to hesitate to go on to the end and continue my horoscope, and said very quickly:

" Your line of life is magnificent, Monsieur; you will live to be sixty at least, but take care not to spend it too freely or to use it immoderately; beware of strong emotions and of any passional crisis, for I remark a gap there in the full vigor of your age, and that gap, that incurable malady which I mentioned to you, in the line of your heart.''

I mastered myself, in order not to smile, and took my leave of her, but everything that she foretold has been realized, and I dare not look at that sinister gap which she saw in my line of life—*for that gap can only mean madness!*

Madness, my poor, dear, adored Elaine!

PART XVIII

I became as bad and spiteful as if the spirit of hatred had possession of me, and envied those whose life was too happy and who had no cares to trouble them. I could not conceal my pleasure when one of those domestic dramas occurred in which hearts bleed and are broken, in which odious treachery and bitter sufferings are brought to light.

I attended divorce proceedings, with their miserable episodes, with the wranglings of the lawyers and all the unhappiness that they revealed, and which exposed the vanity of dreams, the tricks of women, the lowness of some minds, the foul animal that slumbers in most hearts. They attracted me like a delightful play, a piece which rivets one from the first to the last act. I listened greedily to passionate letters, those mad prayers whose secrets some lawyer violates and which he reads aloud in a mocking tone, and which he gives pellmell to the bench and to the public, who have come to be amused or to be excited, and to stare at the victims of love.

I followed those proceedings where unfaithfulness was unfolded chapter by chapter in its brutal reality of things that had actually occurred, and for the first time I forgot my own unhappiness in them. Sometimes the husband and wife were there, as if they wished to defy each other, to meet in some last encounter; and pale and feverish they watched each other, devoured each other with their eyes, hiding their grief and their misery.

It seemed to me as if I were looking at a heap of ruins, or breathing in the odor of an ambulance in which dying men were groaning, and that those unhappy people were assuaging my trouble somewhat and taking their share of it.

I used to read the advertisements in the personal columns in the newspapers, where the same exalted phrases used to recur, where I read the same despairing adieus, earnest requests for a meeting, echoes of past affection, and vain vows; and all this relieved me, vaguely appeased me, and made me think less about myself—that hateful, incurable *I* which I longed to destroy!

PART XIX

As the heat was very oppressive and there was not a breath of wind, after dinner Elaine wanted to go for a drive in the Bois de Boulogne, and we drove in the victoria toward the bridge at Suresnes.

It was getting late, and the dark drives looked like deserted labyrinths and cool retreats where one would have liked to have stopped late, where the very rustle of the leaves seemed to whisper temptations, and there was seduction in the softness of the air and in the infinite music of the silence.

Occasionally lights were to be seen among the trees, and the crescent of the new moon shone like a half-opened gold circlet in the serene sky, and the green sward, the copses and the small lakes, which gave an uncertain reflection of the surrounding objects, came into sight suddenly, out of the shade, and the intoxicating smell of the hay and of the flower beds rose from the earth as if from a sachet.

We did not speak, but the jolts of the carriage occasionally brought us quite close together, and as if I were being attracted by some irresistible force, I turned to Elaine, and saw that her eyes were full of tears and that she was very pale, and my whole body trembled when I looked at her. Suddenly, as if she could not bear this state of affairs any longer, she threw her arms round my neck, and with her lips almost touching mine she said:

"Why do you not love me any longer? Why do you make me so unhappy? What have I done to you, Jacques?"

She was at my mercy, she was undergoing the influence of the charm of one of those moonlight nights which unstring women's nerves, make them languid, and leave them without a will and without any strength, and I thought that was she going to tell me everything and to confess everything to me, and I had to master myself not to kiss her on her sweet, coaxing lips, but I only replied coldly:

"Do you not know, Elaine? Did you not think that sooner or later I should discover everything that you have been trying to hide from me?"

She sat up in terror, and repeated as if she were in a profound stupor:

"What have I been trying to hide from you?"

I had said too much, and was bound to go on to the end and to finish, even though I repented of it ever afterward, and amid the noise of the carriage I said in a hoarse voice:

"Is it not your fault if I have become estranged from you? Shall I be the only one to be unhappy, I who loved you so dearly, who believed in you, and whom you have deceived?"

Elaine closed my mouth with her fingers, and breathing hard, with dilated eyes and with such a pale face that I thought she was going to faint, she said hoarsely:

"Be quiet, be quiet, you are frightening me—frightening me as if you were a madman."

Those words froze me, and I shivered as if some phantoms were appearing among the trees and showing me the place that had been marked out for me by Destiny, and I felt inclined to jump from the carriage and to run to the river, which was calling to me yonder in a maternal voice and inviting me to an eternal sleep, eternal repose, but Elaine called out to the coachman:

"We will go home, Firmin; drive as fast as you can!"

We did not exchange another word, and during the whole drive Elaine sobbed convulsively, though she tried to hide the sound with her pocket-handkerchief, and I understood that it was all finished *and that I had killed our love.*

PART XX

Yes, all was finished, and stupidly finished, without the decisive explanation, in which I should find strength to escape from a hateful yoke, and to repudiate the woman who had allured me with false caresses, and who no longer ought to bear my name.

It was either that, or else—who knows?—the happiness, the peace, the love which was not troubled by any evil afterthoughts, that absolute love that I dreamed of between Elaine and myself when I asked for her hand, and which I was still continually dreaming of with the despair of a condemned soul far from Paradise, and from which I was suffering, and which would kill me.

She prevented me from speaking; with her trembling hand she checked that flow of frenzied words which were about to come from my pained heart, those terrible accusations which an imperious, resistless force incited me to utter, and those terrified words which escaped from her pale lips froze me again, and penetrated to my marrow as if they had been some piercing wind.

In spite of it all, I was in full possession of my reason, I was not in a passion, and I could not have looked like a fool.

What could she have seen unusual in my eyes that frightened her? What inflections were there in my voice for such an idea suddenly to arise in her brain? Suppose she had not made a mistake, suppose I no longer knew what I was saying nor what I was doing, and really had that terrible malady that she had mentioned, and which I cannot repeat!

It seems to me now as if I could see myself in a mirror of anguish, altogether changed, as if my head were a complete void at times and became something sonorous, and then was struck violent, prolonged blows from a heavy clapper, as if it had been a bell, filling it with tumultuous, deafening vibrations from a kind of loud tocsin and from monotonous peals, that were succeeded by the silence of the grave.

And the voice of recollection, a voice which tells me Elaine's mysterious history, which speaks to me only of her, which recalls that initial night, that strange night of happiness and of grief, when I doubted her fidelity, when I doubted her heart as well as I did herself, passes slowly through this silence all at once, like the voice of distant music.

Alas! Suppose she had not made a mistake!

PART XXI

I must be an object of hatred to her, and I left home without writing her a line, without trying to see her, without wishing her good-by. She may pity me or she may hate me, but she certainly does not love me any longer, and I have myself buried that love, for which I would formerly have given my whole life. As she is young and pretty, however, Elaine will soon console herself for these passing troubles with some soul that is the shadow of her own, and will replace me, if she has not done that already, and will seek happiness in new environments.

What are she and her friends plotting? What will they try to do to prevent me from interfering with them? What snares will they set for me so that I may go and end my miserable life in some dungeon from which there is no release?

But that is impossible; it can never be. Elaine belongs to me altogether and forever; she is my property, my chattel, my happiness. I adore her, I want her all to myself, *even though she be guilty,* and I will never leave her again for a moment. I will still cling to her petticoats, I will roll at her feet and ask her pardon, for I thirst for her kisses and her love.

To-night, in a few hours, I shall be with her, I shall go into *our* room, and I will cover the cheeks of my fair-haired darling with such kisses that she will no longer think me mad, and if she cries out, if she defends herself and spurns me, I shall kill her; I have made up my mind to that.

I know that I shall strike her with the Arab knife that is on one of the console tables in our room among other knick-knacks. I see the spot where I shall plunge in the sharp blade, into the nape of her neck, which is covered with little, soft, pale golden curls, that are the same color as the hair of her head. This knife attracted me so at one time, during the chaste period of our engagement, that I used to wish to bite it, as if it had been some fruit. I shall do it some day in the country, when she is bathed in a ray of sunlight, which makes her look dazzling in her pink muslin dress, some day on a towing path, when the nightingales are singing and the dragonflies, with their reflections of blue and silver, are flying about.

There, there I shall skillfully plunge it in up to the hilt, like those who know how to kill.

PART XXII

And after I had killed her, what then?

As the judges would not be able to explain such an extraordinary crime to themselves, they would, of course, say that I was mad; medical men would examine me and would immediately agree that I ought at once to be kept under supervision, taken care of, and placed in a lunatic asylum.

And for years, perhaps, because I was strong, and because such a vigorous animal would survive the calamity intact, although my intellect might give way, I should remain a prey to these chimeras, carry that fixed idea of her lies, her impurity, and her shame about with me, that would be my one recollection, and I should suffer unceasingly.

I am writing all this perfectly coolly and in full possession of my reason; I have perfect prescience of what my resolve entails, and of this blind rush toward death. I feel that my very minutes are numbered, and that I no longer have anything in my skull, in which some fire, though I do not quite know what it is, is burning, except a few particles of what used to be my brain.

Just as a short time ago I should certainly have murdered Elaine if she had been with me when invisible hands seemed to be pushing me toward her, inaudible voices ordered me to commit that murder, it is surely most probable that I shall have another crisis, and will there be any awakening from that?

Ah! It will be a thousand times better, since Destiny has left me a half-open door, to escape from life before it is too late, before the free, sane, strong man that I am at present becomes the most pitiable, the most destructive, the most dangerous of human wrecks!

May all these notes of my misery fall into Elaine's hands some day, may she read them to the end, pity, and absolve me, and for a long time mourn for me!

(*Here ends Jacques's journal.*)

An Artist's Wife

"AH, Monsieur!" said the old juggler, "it is only a matter of practice and habit, that is all. One must, of course, have a little talent in that direction and not be butter-fingered, but what is chiefly necessary is patience and daily practice for long, long years."

His modesty surprised me all the more because he was the cleverest performer of the kind I had ever seen, though most of them are infatuated with their own skill. I had frequently seen him in some circus or other, or even in traveling shows, as had every one, performing the trick that consists of putting a man or woman with extended arms against a wooden target and in throwing knives from a distance between their fingers and round their head. There is nothing very extraordinary in it, after all, when one knows the tricks of the trade, and that the knives are not the least sharp, and stick into the wood at some distance from the flesh. It is the accuracy and the rapidity of the throws, the glitter of the blades, the curve which the handles make toward their living aim which give an air of danger to an exhibition that has become commonplace and only requires very middling skill.

But here there was no trick and no deception and no dust thrown into the eyes. It was done in good earnest and in all sincerity. The knives were as sharp as razors, and the old mountebank planted them close to the flesh, exactly in the angle between the fingers, and surrounded the head with a perfect halo of knives, and the neck with a collar, from which nobody could have extricated himself without cutting his carotid artery, while to increase the difficulty the old fellow went through the performance blindfolded, his whole face being covered with a close mask of thick oilcloth.

Naturally, like other great artists, he was not understood by the crowd, who confounded him with vulgar tricksters, and his mask only appeared to them a trick the more, and a very common trick into the bargain. "He must think us very stupid," they said. "How could he possibly aim without having his eyes open?" And they thought there must be imperceptible holes in the oilcloth, a sort of lattice-work concealed in the material. It was useless for him to allow the public to examine the mask for themselves before the exhibition began. It was all very well that they could not discover any trick, but they were only all the more convinced that they were being tricked. Did not the people know that they ought to be tricked?

I had recognized a great artist in the old juggler, and I was quite sure that he was altogether incapable of any trickery, and I told him so, while expressing my admiration; and he had been touched, both by my admiration and, above all, by the justice I had done him. Thus we became good friends, and he explained to me, very modestly, the real trick which the crowd cannot understand, the eternal trick comprised in these simple words: "To be gifted by nature, and to practice every day for long, long years."

He had been especially struck by my saying that I believed him incapable of trickery. "Yes," he said to me; "quite incapable. Incapable to a degree which you cannot imagine. If I were to tell you! But where would be the use?"

His face clouded over and his eyes filled with tears, but I did not venture to force his confidence. My looks, however, were no doubt not as discreet as my silence, and begged him to speak, and so he responded to their mute appeal. "After all," he said, "why should I not tell you about it? You will understand me." And he added, with a look of sudden ferocity: "She understood it, at any rate!"

"Who?" I asked.

"My faithless wife," he replied. "Ah! Monsieur, what an abominable creature she was, if you only knew! Yes, she understood it too well, too well, and that is why I hate her so; even more on that account than for having deceived me. For that is a natural fault, is it not, and may be pardoned? But the other thing was a crime, a horrible crime."

The woman who stood against the wooden target every night with her arms stretched out and her fingers extended, and whom the old juggler fitted with gloves and with a halo formed of his knives, which were as sharp as razors and which he planted close to her, was his wife. She might have been a woman of forty, and must have been fairly pretty, but with a perverse prettiness. She had an impudent mouth, a mouth that was at the same time sensual and bad, with the lower lip too thick for the thin, dry upper lip.

I had several times noticed that every time he planted a knife in the board she uttered a laugh, so low as scarcely to be heard, but which was very significant when one heard it, for it was a hard and very mocking laugh, but I had always attributed that sort of reply to some artifice which the occasion required. It was intended, I thought, to accentuate the danger she incurred and the contempt that she felt for it, thanks to the sureness of the thrower's hands, and so I was very much surprised when the old man said to me:

"Have you observed her laugh, I say? Her evil laugh, which makes fun of me, and her cowardly laugh, which defies me? Yes, cowardly, because she knows that nothing can happen to her, nothing, in spite of all she deserves, in spite of all that I ought to do to her, in spite of all that I *want* to do to her."

"What do you want to do?"

"Confound it! Cannot you guess? I want to kill her."

"To kill her because she has——"

"Because she has deceived me? No, no, not that, I tell you again. I have forgiven her for that, a long time ago, and I am too much accustomed to it! But the worst of it is that the first time I forgave her, when I told her that, all the same, I might some day have my revenge by cutting her throat, if

I chose, without seeming to do it on purpose, as if it were an accident, mere awkwardness——"

"Oh! So you said that to her?"

"Of course I did, and I meant it. I thought I might be able to do it, for, you see, I had the perfect right to do so. It was so simple, so easy, so tempting! Just think! A mistake of less than half an inch and her skin would be cut at the neck where the jugular vein is, and the jugular would be severed. My knives cut very well! And when once the jugular is cut—good-by! The blood would spurt out, one, two, three red jets, and all would be over; she would be dead, and I should have had my revenge!"

"That is true, certainly, horribly true!"

"And without any risk to me, eh? An accident, that is all; bad luck, one of those mistakes which happen every day in our business. What could they accuse me of? Accidental homicide, that would be all! They would even pity me, rather than accuse me. 'My wife! My poor wife!' I should say, sobbing. 'My wife, who is so necessary to me, who is half the bread-winner, who takes part in my performance!' You must acknowledge that I should be pitied!"

"Certainly; there is no doubt about that."

"And you must allow that such a revenge would be a very nice revenge, the best possible revenge which I could have with impunity?"

"Evidently that is so."

"Very well! But when I told her so, just as I have told you, only more forcibly, threatening her, as I was mad with rage and ready to do the deed that I had dreamed of, on the spot, what do you think she said?"

" That you were a good fellow, and would certainly not have the atrocious courage to——"

" Tut! tut! tut! I am not such a good fellow as you think. I am not afraid of blood, and that I have proved already, though it would be useless to tell you how and where. But I had no need to prove it to her, for she knows that I am capable of a good many things, even of crime, especially of a crime——"

" And she was not frightened? "

" No. She merely replied that I could not do what I said; you understand. That I could not do it! "

" Why not? "

" Ah! Monsieur, so you do not understand? Why do you not? Have I not explained to you by what constant, long daily practice I have learned to plant my knives without seeing what I am doing? "

" Yes; well, what then? "

" Well! Cannot you understand what she has understood with such terrible results, that now my hand would no longer obey me if I wished to make a mistake as I threw? "

" Is it possible? "

" Nothing is truer, I am sorry to say. For I really have wished to have my revenge, which I have dreamed of and which I thought so easy. Exasperated by that bad woman's insolence and confidence in her own safety, I have several times made up my mind to kill her, and have exerted all my energy and all my skill to make my knives fly aside when I threw them to make a border round her neck. I tried with all my might to make them deviate half an inch, just enough to cut her throat. I wanted to, and I have never succeeded, never. And always the creature's horrible laugh makes fun of me, always, always."

And with a deluge of tears, with something like a roar of unsatiated and muzzled rage, he ground his teeth as he wound up: "She knows me, the jade; she is in the secret of my work, of my patience, of my trick, routine, whatever you may call it! She lives in my innermost being, and sees into it more closely than you do, or than I do myself. She knows what a faultless machine I have become, the machine of which she makes fun, the machine which is too well wound up, the machine which cannot get out of order, and she knows that I *cannot* make a mistake."

On Cats

I WAS sitting, the other day, on a bench outside of my door, with the sun shining full upon me, a basket of blooming anemones in front of me, reading a book that had recently appeared, a good book, a rare thing, and also a delightful book, *Le Tonnelier,* by Georges Duval. A large white cat, which belonged to the gardener, jumped on my knees, by the shock of its impact closing the book, which I laid beside me, to caress the beast.

It was hot; the odor of young flowers, a shy, light, intermittent odor, floated in the air, and I also felt passing breaths of cold coming from those great white peaks that I saw in the distance.

But the sun was scorching, penetrating, with that heat which digs down into the earth and makes it alive, which splits the seeds in order to animate the sleeping germs within, and slits the buds, so that the young leaves may come out. The cat was rolling on its back, on my knees, with its paws extended, clawing the air, showing its pointed teeth inside of its lips, and its green eyes peeping out through the slit of its half-closed lids. I patted and caressed the soft and nervous animal, supple as a piece of silk, gentle, warm, delicious, and dangerous. She was purring delightedly, and ready to bite, for she likes to claw, as well as to be caressed. She stretched and turned her neck, and when I stopped touching her, she sat up and passed her head under my raised hand.

I made her nervous and she made me nervous, too, for I both love and detest these charming and perfidious animals. It gives me pleasure to touch them, to pass my hand over their silky, crackling fur, to feel their warmth through the fine, exquisite texture of their coat. There is nothing softer than the warm and vibrant hair of a cat, and nothing imparts to the skin a more delicate, refined, and rare sensation. But this living coat makes my fingers itch with a strange and fierce desire to strangle the beast that I am caressing. I feel in her the inclination that she has to bite me and to tear me. I feel and I catch this inclination, like a fluid which she communicates to me; I catch it from this warm skin through the tips of my fingers, and it creeps along my nerves, along my limbs, up to my heart, up to my head; it fells me, it runs along my skin, and it makes me clinch my teeth. And all the while I feel at the tips of my ten fingers the light, lively tickling which penetrates and suffuses my body.

And if the beast begins, if she bites me or claws me, I take her by the neck, give a turn, and fling her away like a sling-stone, so quickly and so brutally that she never has the time to get even with me.

I remember that, even as a child, I loved cats, but yet with the brusque desire to strangle them in my little hands. One day I suddenly saw, at the far end of the garden, on the edge of the woods, something gray that was rolling over in the tall grass. I ran down to see; it was a cat caught in a trap, that was strangling, with the death-rattle in its throat. It was twisting its body, clawing the earth round it, jumping up, and falling down; and then it began all over again, and its quick, hoarse breathing sounded like the noise of a pump, a dreadful noise that is still ringing in my ears.

I might have taken a spade and cut the trap; I might have run for our man-servant, or I might have gone to tell my father. But, no; I did not stir from the spot, and with beating heart and trembling and cruel joy I watched it die; for it was a cat. Had it been a dog I should have cut the wire string with my teeth, rather than let it suffer a moment longer.

And when the cat was dead, quite dead, and still warm, I went up to touch it and pull its tail.

Yet they are delicious, especially when, in caressing them, they rub against our skin, purr, and roll over us, looking at us with their yellow eyes which never seem to see us, and it is then that we feel the insecurity of their caresses, the perfidious egoism of their pleasure.

Women also give us this sensation, charming, gentle women, with clear and false eyes, who have chosen us in order to get a taste of love. With them, when they open their arms, with pursed-up lips, when one presses them close, with beating heart, when one tastes the sweet, sensual joy of their tender caress, one feels very well that one is holding a cat, a cat with claws and nails, a perfidious, sly, amorous, hostile cat, who will bite when she is tired of kissing.

All the poets have loved cats. Baudelaire has sung of them divinely.

"Les amoureux fervents et les savants austères

One day I had the strange sensation of having lived in the enchanted palace of the White Cat, a magical château, where ruled one of these sinuous, mysterious, troublous beasts, perhaps the only one of all the beings whose footfall one never hears.

It was last summer, on the same coast of the Mediterranean. There was a fierce heat at Nice, and I asked if the people here did not have somewhere in the mountain above a cool valley, where they could go for a breath of fresh air.

They told me of the valley of Thorence. I wanted to see it. I must first go to Grasse, the city of perfumes, of which I shall speak some day, describing how they make those essences and quintessences of flowers, which are worth up to two thousand francs a liter. I passed the evening and the night in an old hotel in the city, a second-class inn, where the quality of the food was as doubtful as the cleanness of the rooms. I left in the morning.

The route lay through the mountains, skirting deep ravines, with sharp, sterile, and wild peaks rising up on the sides. I was wondering to what a curious summer place I had been sent, and I was on the point of turning back to get to Nice that same evening, when I suddenly perceived in front of me, on a mountain which seemed to shut off the entire valley, an immense and splendid ruin, with its towers and crumbled walls outlined against the sky, a curious heap of a dead fortress. It was the remains of an ancient priory of the Knights

Templars, who formerly held sway in the country of Thorence.

Skirting this mountain, I suddenly discovered a long green valley, fresh and restful. In the bottom there were meadows, running water, and willows, and on the slope pines were climbing up to the sky.

Opposite the priory, on the further side of the valley, but lower, there stands the Château of Quatre Tours, which was built about 1530, and is still inhabited. Its architecture does not yet show any trace of the Renaissance.

It is a heavy and well-built pile of masonry, very strong in appearance, and flanked by four watch-towers, as its name indicates.

I had a letter of introduction to the owners of this manor, who would not let me go on to the hotel.

The whole valley, which is really delightful, is one of the most charming summer places that one can imagine.

I went first through a kind of salon, the walls of which are covered by old Cordova leather, then through another room, where, by the light of my candle, I caught a glimpse of old portraits of ladies on the walls, those pictures of which Théophile Gautier has said:

> "I love to see you in your oval frames,
> Yellow portraits of the beauties of old,
> Holding withering roses in your hands,
> As is fitting for century-old flowers."

Then I entered the room in which I was to sleep.

I turned to examine it as soon as I was alone. It was hung with old painted tapestries, showing pink towers against blue backgrounds, and large, fantastic birds under foliage of precious stones.

My dressing-room was in one of the towers. The windows, which were cut large into the wall on the inside, sloped through the masonry, narrowing as they went out toward the daylight, being, in fact, nothing more than portholes, openings through which men on the outside were killed. I closed my door, lay down, and went to sleep.

And I dreamed; one always dreams somewhat of that through which he has passed during the day. I was traveling; I entered an inn, where I saw at a table before the fire a servant in gala livery and a mason, a curious fellowship, but which did not astonish me. They were talking of Victor Hugo, who had just died, and I took part in their conversation. I finally went to bed in a room whose door did not close, and suddenly I saw the servant and the mason tiptoeing toward my bed, armed with bricks.

I started out of my sleep, and it took me some minutes to collect myself. Then I recalled the events of the day before my arrival at Thorence, the *châtelain's* amiable reception. . . . I was about to close my eyes when I saw—yes, I saw in the darkness of the night, in the middle of my room, at about the height of a man's head, two fiery eyes looking at me.

I reached for a match, and while I was striking it I heard a noise, a slight, soft noise, like that of the dropping of a damp roll of cloth, and when I had made a light I saw nothing but a large table in the middle of the apartment.

I got up. I went through the two rooms, looked under my bed and into the closets, but found noth-

I thought, therefore, that I had continued to dream for a few seconds after being awake, and I went to sleep again, not without some difficulty.

Again I began to dream. This time, also, I was traveling, but in the East, the land that I love, and I came to a Turk who was living in the open desert. He was a splendid Turk; not an Arab, but a Turk, large, amiable, charming, dressed in Turkish fashion, with a turban and a whole assortment of silks on his back, a real Turk of the Théâtre Français, who made me compliments in offering me sweets, on a delicious divan.

Then a small negro boy led me to my room—so all my dreams finished there—a perfumed, sky-blue room, with skins on the floor, and before the fire—the idea of fire pursued me even to the desert—sat a scantily clad woman in a low chair, who was expecting me.

She was of the most pure Oriental type, with stars on the cheeks, the forehead, and chin, immense eyes, an admirable body, a little brown but warm and captivating.

She looked at me, and I thought: "This is what I call hospitality. It is not in our stupid land of the North, our land of inept prudishness and odious shamefacedness and imbecile morality, where one would receive a stranger in this fashion."

I went up to her and spoke, but she replied only by signs, not knowing a word of my language, which my Turk, her master, knew so well.

All the more happy in that she would be silent, I took her by the hand and led her to my couch, where I lay down beside her. . . . But one always awakens just at that point! So I woke up, and I was not very much surprised to feel something soft and warm under my hand, which I caressed amorously.

Then, on gathering together my thoughts, I saw that it was a cat, a large cat, snuggled up against my cheek, which slept undisturbed. I let it lie, and, following its example, went to sleep once more.

When day broke it was gone, and I really thought that I had been dreaming, for I did not understand how she could have come into my room and gone out again, the door being locked.

When I told my adventure (not all of it) to my amiable host, he began to laugh, and said: "He came in through the cat-hole," and, lifting up a curtain, he showed me a small, round black hole in the wall.

And I learned that almost all the old habitations in this country have such long, narrow passages through the walls, which go from the cellar to the garret, from the maid-servant's room to that of the master, and which constitute the cat the king and the master of the house.

He goes about as he likes, visiting his domain at his pleasure; he can sleep in all the beds, see everything and hear everything, know all the secrets, all the habits, and all the shame of the house. He is everywhere at home, and can enter everywhere, the animal that goes about noiselessly, the silent prowler, the midnight promenader of hollow walls.

And I thought of a stanza of Baudelaire's:

> "He is the homely spirit of the spot;
> As judge he sees us all, and doth inspire
> All things that pass in his domain;
> Perhaps he is a fay—perhaps a god."

Countess Satan

THEY were discussing dynamite, the social revolution, nihilism; and even those who cared least about politics had something to say. Some were alarmed, others philosophized, while others again tried to smile.

"Bah!" said N——, "when we are all blown up we shall see what it is like. Perhaps, after all, it may be an amusing sensation, provided one ascends enough."

"But we shall not be blown up at all," said G——, the optimist, interrupting him. "It is all a romance."

"You are mistaken, my dear fellow," replied Jules de C——. "It sounds like a romance, but with that confounded nihilism, everything seems like one, though it would be a mistake to trust to it. Take myself, for instance, the manner in which I made Bakounine's acquaintance . . ."

They knew that he was a good narrator, and it was no secret that his life had been an adventurous one, so they drew closer to him, and listened with interest. This is what he told them:

"I met Countess Nioska W——, that strange woman who was usually called Countess Satan, in Naples; I immediately attached myself to her out of curiosity, and soon fell in love with her. Not that she was beautiful, for she was a Russian who had all the bad characteristics of the Russian type. She was thin and squat at the same time, while her face was sallow and puffy, with high cheek-bones and a Cossack nose. But her conversation bewitched every one.

"She was many-sided, learned, a philosopher, scientifically depraved, satanic. Perhaps the word is rather pretentious, but it exactly expresses what I want to say; for, in other words, she loved evil for the sake of evil. She rejoiced in other people's vices, and liked to sow the seeds of evil, in order to see it flourish. And that on a fraudulent, on an enormous scale. It was not enough for her to corrupt individuals; she only did that to keep her hand in; what she wished to do was to corrupt the masses. By slightly altering it after her own fashion, she might have adopted the famous saying of Caligula. She also wished that the whole human race had but one head; but not in order that she might cut it off, but that she might make the philosophy of nihilism flourish there.

"What a temptation to become the lord and master of such a monster! And I allowed myself to be tempted and undertook the adventure. The means came unsought-for by me, and the only thing that I had to do was to show myself more perverted and satanical than she was herself. And so I played the devil.

" 'Yes,' I said, 'we writers are the best instruments for doing evil, as our books may be bottles of poison. The so-called men of action only turn the handle of the *mitrailleuse* which we have loaded. Formulas will destroy the world, and it is we who invent them.'

" 'That is true,' she said, 'and that is what is lacking in Bakounine, I am sorry to say.'

" That name was constantly in her mouth, and so I asked her for details, which she gave me, as she knew the man intimately.

" 'After all,' she said, with a contemptuous grimace, 'he is only a kind of Garibaldi.'

" She told me, although she made fun of him as she did so, about his Odyssey of the barricades and of the hulks which made up Bakounine's legion, and which is, nevertheless, only the exact truth; his part as leader of the insurgents at Prague and then at Dresden; his first death sentence; about his imprisonment at Olmütz and in the casemates of the fortress of St. Peter and St. Paul; in a subterranean dungeon at Schüsselburg; about his exile to Siberia and his wonderful escape down the River Amoor on a Japanese coasting vessel, by way of Yokohama and San Francisco; and about his final arrival in London, whence he was directing all the operations of nihilism.

" 'You see,' she said, 'he is a thorough adventurer, and now all his adventures are over. He got married at Tobolsk and became a mere respectable, middle-class man. And then he has no individual ideas. Herzen, the pamphleteer of Kolokol, inspired him with the only fertile phrase that he ever uttered: *Land and Liberty!* But that is not yet the definite formula, the general formula; what I will call the dynamite formula. At best, Bakounine would become an incendiary and burn down cities. And what is that, I ask you? Bah! A second-hand Rostopchin! He needs a prompter, and I offered to become his prompter, but he did not take me seriously.'

* * * * * * *

"It would be useless to enter into all the psychological details which marked the course of my passion for the Countess, and to explain to you more fully the attraction of curiosity which she offered me more and more every day. It was becoming exasperating, and the more so as she resisted me as stoutly as the shyest of innocents could have done; but at the end of a month I saw what her game was. Do you know what she had thought of? She meant to make me Bakounine's prompter, or, at any rate, that is what she said. But no doubt she reserved the right to herself—and that is how I understood her—to prompt the prompter, and my passion for her, which she purposely left unsatisfied, assured her that absolute power over me.

"All this may appear madness to you, but it is, nevertheless, the exact truth, and, in short, one morning she bluntly made the offer: 'Become Bakounine's soul, and you shall have me.'

"Of course I accepted, for it was too fantastically strange to refuse; don't you think so? What an adventure! What luck! A number of letters between the Countess and Bakounine prepared the way; I was introduced to him at his house, and they discussed me there. I became a sort of Western prophet, a mystic charmer who was ready to annihilate the Latin races, the Saint Paul of the new religion of nothingness; and at last a day was fixed for us to meet in London. He lived in a small one-storied house in Pimlico, with a tiny garden in front, and nothing remarkable about it.

"We were first of all shown into the ordinary parlor of all English homes, and then upstairs. The room into which the Countess and I were ushered was small and very badly furnished, with a square table with writing materials on it in the center of the room. That was his sanctuary; the deity soon appeared, and I saw him in flesh and bone; especially in flesh, for he was enormously stout. His broad face, with prominent cheek-bones, in spite of the fat; his nose like a double funnel, and his small, sharp eyes, which had a magnetic look, proclaimed the Tartar, the old Turanian blood which produced the Attilas, the Gengis-Khans, the Tamerlanes. The obesity which is characteristic of the nomad races, who are always on horseback or driving, added to his Asiatic look. The man was certainly not a European, a slave, a descendant of the deistic Aryans, but a descendant of the atheistic hordes who had several times already almost overrun Europe, and who, instead of any ideas of progress, have the belief in nihilism at the bottom of their heart.

"I was astonished, for I had not expected that the majesty of a whole race could be thus revived in a man, and my stupefaction increased after an hour's conversation. I could quite understand why such a Colossus had not wished for the Countess as his Egeria; she was a mere silly child to have dreamed of acting such a part to such a thinker. She had not felt the profoundness of the horrible philosophy which was hidden under that material activity, nor had she seen the prophet under that man of the barricades. Or, perhaps, he had not thought it advisable to reveal himself to her; but he revealed himself to me, and inspired me with terror.

"A prophet? Oh, yes! He thought himself an Attila, and foresaw the consequences of his revolution; it was not only from instinct but also from theory that he urged a nation on to nihilism. The phrase is not his, but Tourgueneff's, I believe, but the idea certainly belongs to him. He got his program of agricultural communism from Herzen, and his destructive radicalism from Pougatcheff, but he did not stop there. I mean that he went on to evil for the sake of evil. Herzen wished for the happiness of the Slav peasant; Pougatcheff wanted to be elected Emperor, but all that Bakounine wanted was to overthrow the actual order of things, no matter by what means, and to replace the social order by a universal upheaval.

"It was the dream of a Tartar; it was true nihilism pushed to its extreme practical conclusion. It was, in a word, the applied philosophy of chance, the indeterminate aim of anarchy. Monstrous it may be, but grand in its monstrosity.

"And you must note that the man of action so despised by the Countess became in Bakounine the gigantic dreamer whom I have just shown to you, and his dream did not remain a dream, but began to be realized. It was through Bakounine's efforts that the nihilistic party became an organization, an organization comprising all forms of opinion, but on the whole a formidable organization, whose advance guard is true nihilism, the object of which is nothing less than to destroy the Western world, to see it blossom from under the ruins of a general dispersion, which is the last conception of modern Tartarism.

"I never saw Bakounine again, for the Countess's conquest would have been too dearly bought by any attempt to act a comedy with this Old Man of the Mountains. And, besides that, after this visit, poor Countess Satan appeared to me quite silly. Her famous Satanism was nothing but the flicker of a spirit-lamp, and she had certainly had not shown much intelligence when she could not understand that prodigious monster. And as she had attracted me only by her intellect and her perversity, I was disgusted as soon as she laid aside that mask. I left her without telling her of my intention, and never saw her again.

"No doubt they both took me for a spy from the Third Section of the Imperial Chancellery. In that case, they must have thought me very strong to have resisted, and all I have to do is to beware, if any affiliated members of their society should happen to recognize me! . . ."

Then he smiled and, turning to the waiter who had just come in, he said: "Meanwhile, open us another bottle of champagne, and make the cork pop! It will, at any rate, somewhat accustom us to the day when we ourselves shall all be blown up with dynamite."

Crash

LOVE is stronger than death, and consequently, also, than the greatest financial catastrophe.

A young and by no means bad-looking son of Palestine, and one of the barons of the Almanac of the Ghetto, who had left the field covered with wounds in the last general engagement on the Stock Exchange, used to go very frequently to the Universal Exhibition in Vienna in 1873, in order to divert his thoughts, and to console himself amid the varied scenes and the numerous objects of attraction there. One day he met in the Russian section a newly married couple, who had a very old coat-of-arms, but on the other hand a very modest income.

This latter circumstance had frequently emboldened the stockbroker to make secret overtures to the delightful little lady, overtures which might have fascinated certain Viennese actresses, but which were sure to insult a respectable woman. The Baroness, whose name appeared in the Almanach de Gotha, therefore felt something very like hatred for the man from the Ghetto, and for a long time her pretty little head had been full of various plans of revenge.

The stockbroker, who was really and even passionately in love with her, got close to her in the Exhibition buildings, which he could do all the more easily, since the little woman's husband had taken to flight, foreseeing mischief, as soon as she went up to the showcase of a Russian fur dealer, before which she remained standing in rapture.

"Do look at that lovely fur," the Baroness said, while her dark eyes expressed her pleasure; "I must have it."

But she looked at the white ticket on which the price was marked.

"Four thousand roubles," she said in despair; "that is about six thousand florins."

"Certainly," he replied, "but what of that? It is a sum not worth mentioning in the presence of such a charming lady."

"But my husband is not in a position——"

"Be less cruel than usual for once," the man from the Ghetto said to the young woman in a low voice, "and allow me to lay this sable skin at your feet."

"I presume that you are joking."

"Not I——"

"I think you must be joking, as I cannot think that you intend to insult me."

"But, Baroness, I love you——"

"That is one reason more why you should not make me angry."

"But——"

"Oh! I am in such a rage," the energetic little woman said; "I could flog you as the 'Venus in Fur' flogged her slave."

"Let me be your slave," the Stock Exchange Baron replied ardently, "and I will gladly put up with everything from you. Really, in this sable cloak, and with a whip in your hand, you would make a most lovely picture of the heroine of that story."

The Baroness looked at the man for a moment with a peculiar smile.

"Then if I were to listen to you favorably, you would let me flog you?" she said after a pause.

"With pleasure."

"Very well," she replied quickly. "You will let me give you twenty-five cuts with a whip, and may command me after the twenty-fifth blow."

"Are you in earnest?"

"Fully."

The man from the Ghetto took her hand and pressed it ardently to his lips.

"When may I come?"

"To-morrow evening at eight o'clock."

"And I may bring the sable cloak and the whip with me?"

"No, I will see about that myself."

The next evening the enamored stockbroker came to the house of the charming little Baroness, and found her alone, lying on a couch, wrapped in a dark fur, while she held a dog whip in her small hand, which the man from the Ghetto kissed.

"You know our agreement," she began.

"Of course I do," the Stock Exchange Baron replied. "I am to allow you to give me twenty-five cuts with the whip, and after the twenty-fifth you will listen to me."

"Yes, but I am going to tie your hands first."

The amorous Baron quietly allowed this new Delilah to tie his hands behind him, and then at her bidding, he knelt down before her, and she raised her whip and hit him hard.

"Oh! That hurts me most confoundedly," he exclaimed.

"I mean it to hurt you," she said, with a mocking laugh, and went on thrashing him without mercy. At last the poor fool groaned with pain, but he consoled himself with the thought that each blow brought him nearer to his happiness.

At the twenty-fourth cut she stopped.

"That only makes twenty-four," the beaten would-be Don Juan remarked.

"I will make you a present of the twenty-fifth," she said, with a laugh.

"And now you are mine, altogether mine," he exclaimed ardently.

"What are you thinking of?"

"Have I not let you beat me?"

"Certainly; but I promised you to grant your wish after the twenty-fifth blow, and you have only received twenty-four," the cruel little bit of virtue cried, "and I have witnesses to prove it."

With these words she drew back the curtains over the door, and her husband, followed by two other gentlemen, came out of the next room, smiling. For a moment the stockbroker remained speechless on his knees before the beautiful woman; then he gave a deep sigh, and sadly uttered that one most significant word:

"Crash!"

A Deer Park In the Provinces

A HUNGARIAN Prince in an Austrian cavalry regiment was stationed, not long ago, in a wealthy Austrian garrison town. The ladies of the local aristocracy naturally did everything they could to ensnare the newcomer, who was young, good-looking, animated, and amusing, and at last one of the mature beauties, who was now resting on her laurels, after innumerable victories in the fervid atmosphere of Viennese society, succeeded in taking him in her toils, but only for a short time, for she had very nearly reached the age where, on the man's side, love ceases and esteem begins. But she had more sense than most women, and she recognized the fact in good time; and, as she did not wish to give up so easily the leading rôle which she played in society, she reflected as to what means she could employ to bind him to her in another manner. It is well known that the notorious Marquise de Pompadour, who was one of the mistresses of Louis XV of France, when her own charms did not suffice to fetter that changeable monarch, conceived the idea of securing the chief power in the State and in society for herself by having a pavilion in the deer park which belonged to her, and where Louis XV was in the habit of hunting, fitted up with every accommodation of a harem, where she brought beautiful women and girls of all ranks of life to the arms of her royal lover.

Inspired by that historical example, the Baroness began to arrange evening parties, balls, and private theatricals in the winter, and in the summer excursions into the country, and thus she gave the Prince, who at that time was still, so to say, at her feet, the opportunity of plucking fresh flowers. But even this clever expedient did not avail in the long run, for beautiful women were scarce in that provincial town, and the few which the local aristocracy could produce were not able to offer the Prince any fresh attractions, when he had made their closer acquaintance. At last, therefore, he turned his back on the highborn Messalinas, and began to bestow marked attention on the pretty women and girls of the middle classes, either in the streets or when he was in his box at the theater.

There was one girl in particular, the daughter of a well-to-do merchant, who was supposed to be the most beautiful girl in the capital, on whom his opera-glass was constantly leveled, and whom he even followed occasionally without being noticed. But Baroness Pompadour soon got wind of this unprincely taste, and determined to do everything in her power to keep her lover and the whole nobility, which was threatened by such an unheard-of disgrace as an intrigue of a Prince with a girl of the middle classes.

"It is really sad," the outraged Baroness once said to me, "that in these days princes and monarchs choose their favorites only from the stage, or even from the scum of the people. But it is the fault of our ladies themselves. They mistake their vocation! Ah! Where are those delightful times when the daughters of the first families looked upon it as an honor to become their Princes' mistresses?" Consequently, the horror of the blue-blooded aristocratic lady was intense when the Prince, in his usual amiable, careless manner, suggested to her to people her deer park with girls of the lower orders.

"It is a ridiculous prejudice," the Prince said on that occasion, "which obliges us to shut ourselves off from the other ranks, and to confine ourselves altogether to our own circle, for monotony and boredom are the inevitable consequences of it. How many honorable men of sense and education, and especially how many charming women and girls, there are, who do not belong to the aristocracy, who would infuse fresh life and a new charm into our dull, listless society! I very much wish that a lady like you would make a beginning, and would give up this exclusiveness, which cannot be maintained in these days, and would enrich our circle with the charming daughters of middle-class families."

A wish of the Prince's was as good as a command; so the Baroness made a wry face, but she accommodated herself to circumstances, and promised to invite some of the prettiest girls of the plebeians to a ball in a few days. She really issued a number of invitations, and even condescended to drive to the house of each of them in person. "But

I must ask one thing of you," she said to each of the pretty girls, "and that is to come dressed as simply as possible; wash muslins will be best. The Prince dislikes all finery and ostentation, and he would be very vexed with me if I were the cause of any extravagance on your part."

The great day arrived; it was quite an event for the little town, and all classes of society were in a state of the greatest excitement. The pretty plebeian girls, with her whom the Prince had first noticed at their head, appeared in all their innocence, in plain wash dresses, according to the Prince's orders, with their hair plainly dressed and without any ornaments except their own fresh, buxom charms. When they were all captives in the den of the proud, aristocratic lioness, the poor little mice were very much terrified when suddenly the aristocratic ladies came into the ballroom, rustling in a sea of silk and lace, with their haughty heads changed into so many hanging gardens of Semiramis, loaded with all the treasures of India and radiant as the sun.

At first the poor girls looked down in shame and confusion, and Baroness Pompadour's eyes glistened with all the joy of triumph, but her ill-natured pleasure did not last long, for the intrigue on which the Prince's ignoble passions were to be shipwrecked recoiled on the highborn lady patroness of the deer park.

It was not the aristocratic ladies in their magnificent toilets that threw the girls of the middle class into the shade, but, on the contrary, those pretty girls in their wash dresses, who with the plain but splendid ornament of their abundant hair looked far more charming than they would have done in silk dresses with long trains, and with flowers in their hair, and the novelty and unwontedness of their appearance there, allured not only the Prince, but all the other gentlemen and officers, so that the proud granddaughters of the lions, griffins, and eagles were quite neglected by the gentlemen, who danced almost exclusively with the pretty girls of the middle class.

The faded lips of the baronesses and countesses uttered many a "For shame!" but all in vain; neither was it any use for the Baroness to make up her mind that she would never again put a social medley before the Prince in her drawing-room, for he had seen through her intrigue, and gave ber up altogether. *Sic transit gloria mundi!*

She, however consoled herself as best she could.

A Fashionable Woman

ALTHOUGH it is easy to show that Austria is far richer in men of genius in every domain than Northern Germany, yet, lacking any special technical training, very few of them become more than mere *dilettanti.* They receive, however, the same systematic military education for their chosen vocation as do the Prussian soldiers.

Leo Wolfram was one of those intellectual *dilettanti,* and the more pleasure one took in his material characters, which were usually taken bodily from real life, and in a certain political, and what is still more, in a plastic plot, the more he was obliged to regret that he had never learned to compose, or to delineate character, or to write; in one word, that he had never become a literary artist. That he had in him the making of a master in the art of narration is proved by his *Dissolving Views* and by his *Goldkind.*

Goldkind, the heroine, is a striking type of our modern society, and the novel contains all the elements of a classic novel, although in a crude, unfinished state. How exactly Leo Wolfram portrayed the conditions of our society is shown in the following reminiscences in which an Austrian woman plays the chief part.

It may be about ten years ago that every day four stylishly dressed persons, who caused much comment there and elsewhere, dined at a table in one corner of the small dining-room of one of the best hotels in Vienna. They were an Austrian landowner, his charming wife, and two young diplomatists, one of whom came from the North while the other was a son of the South. There was no doubt that the lady was the center of general interest.

The practised and discriminating observer of human nature easily recognized in her one of those characters which Goethe has so aptly named "enigmatical." They are always dissatisfied and at variance with themselves and the world, are a riddle to themselves, and can never be relied on. With those interesting and captivating, though unfortunate, contradictions in her nature, she made a strong impression on everybody, even by her mere outward appearance. She was one of those women who are called beautiful, without being really so. Her face, as well as her figure, was lacking in esthetic lines, but there was no doubt that, in spite of that, or perhaps on that very account, she was the most dangerous, fascinating woman that one could imagine.

She was tall and thin, with a certain hardness about her figure which became a charm through the vivacity and grace of her movements; her features harmonized with her figure, for she had a high, clever, cold forehead, a strong mouth with sensual lips, and an angular, sharp chin, the effect of which was, however, diminished by her slightly tilted small nose, her beautifully arched eyebrows, and her large, animated, liquid blue eyes.

In her face, which was almost too expressive for a woman, there was as much feeling, kindness, and candor as there was calculation, coolness, and deceit, and when she was angry and drew her upper lip up, so as to show her dazzlingly white teeth, it had even a devilish look of wickedness and cruelty. She had strikingly beautiful long chestnut hair, which she wore braided and wound like a coronet on top of her head. Besides this, she was remarkable for her elegant taste in dress and a bearing which combined with the dignity of a lady of rank that undefinable something which makes actresses and women of the higher *demi-monde* so interesting to us.

In Paris her respectability would have been questioned, but in Vienna the best drawing-rooms were open to her, and she was not looked upon as more or as less respectable than any other aristocratic beauties.

Her husband decidedly belonged to that class of men whom that witty writer, Balzac, so delightfully calls *les hommes prédestinés* in his *Physiologie du Mariage*. Without doubt he was a very good-looking man, but he bore that stamp of insignificance which so often conceals coarseness and vulgarity, and was one of those men who, in the long run, become unendurable to a woman of refined tastes. He had a good private income, but his wife understood the art of enjoying life, and a deficit in the yearly accounts of the young couple became the rule, without causing the lively lady to check her aristocratic tastes in the least on that account; she kept horses and carriages, was a fine horsewoman, had her box at the opera, and gave delightful little suppers, which at that time was the highest aim of a Viennese woman of her class.

One of the two young diplomats who accompanied her, a young Count belonging to a well-known family in North Germany, a gentleman in the highest sense of the word, was looked upon as her devoted admirer, while the other, who was his most intimate friend in spite of his ancient name and his position as *attaché* of a foreign legation, gave people that vivid impression that he was an adventurer which makes the police keep such a careful eye on some persons; he had also the reputation of being an unscrupulous and dangerous duelist. Short, thin, with a yellow complexion, with strongly marked but interesting features, an aquiline nose, and bright dark eyes, he was the typical picture of an unscrupulous flirt and duelist.

The handsome woman appeared to be *éprise* with the Count, and to take an interest in his friend; at least that was the construction that the others in the dining-room put upon the situation, as far as could be construed from the behavior and looks of the people concerned, and especially from their looks, for the beautiful woman's blue eyes rested on the Count with affection and ardor, and on the Italian from time to time with wild, diabolical sympathy, and it was hard to guess whether there was more love or hatred in that glance. None of the four, however, who were now dining and chatting so gayly together, had any presentiment at the time that they were amusing themselves over a mine, which might explode at any moment and bury them.

It was the husband of the beautiful woman who provided the tinder. One day he told her that she must make up her mind to the most rigid retrenchment, give up her box at the opera, and sell her carriage and horses, if she did not wish to risk her whole position in society. Her creditors had lost all patience, and were threatening to distrain on her property, and even to put her in prison. She made no reply to this revelation, but during dinner she said to the Count, in a whisper, that she must speak to him later, and would, therefore, come to see him at his house. When it was dark she came thickly veiled, and after she had responded to his demonstrations of affection for some time with more patience than amiability, she began. Their conversation is extracted from his diary.

"You are so unconcerned and happy, while misery and disgrace are threatening me!"

"Please explain what you mean!"

"I have incurred some debts."

"Again?" he said reproachfully. "Why do you not come to me at once, for you must do it in the end, and then at least you would avoid exposure?"

"Please do not take me to task," she replied; "you know it only makes me angry. I want some money; can you give me some?"

"How much do you want?" She hesitated, for she had not the courage to name the real amount, but at last she said, in a low voice: "Five thousand florins." It was evidently only a small portion of what she really required, so he replied: "I am sure you want more than that!"

"No."

"Really not?"

"Do not make me angry."

He shrugged his shoulders, went to his strong-box, and gave her the money, whereupon she nodded, and, giving him her hand, she said: "You are always kind, and as long as I have you I am not afraid; but if I were to lose you I should be the most unhappy woman in the world."

"You always have the same fears; but I shall never leave you; it would be impossible for me to separate from you," the Count exclaimed.

"And if you die?" she interrupted him hastily.

"If I die?" the Count said, with a peculiar smile. "I have provided for you in that event, also."

"Do you mean to say——" she stammered, flushed, and her beautiful large eyes rested on her lover with an indescribable expression in them. He, however, opened a drawer in his writing table and took out a document, which he gave to her. It was his will. She opened it with almost indecent haste, and when she saw the amount—thirty thousand florins—she grew pale to her very lips.

It was a moment in which the germ of a crime was sown in her breast, but one of those crimes which cannot be touched by the Criminal Code. A few days after she had paid her visit to the Count she herself received one from the Italian. In the course of conversation he took a jewel case out of his breast pocket and asked her opinion of the ornaments, as she was well known for her taste in such matters, telling her at the same time that it was intended as a present for an actress whom he admired.

"It is a magnificent set!" she said, as she looked at it. "You have made an excellent selection." Then she suddenly became absorbed in thought, while her nostrils began to quiver, and that touch of cold cruelty played on her lips.

"Do you think that the lady for whom this ornament is intended will be pleased with it?" the Italian asked.

"Certainly," she replied; "I myself would give a great deal to own it."

"Then may I venture to offer it to you?" the Italian said.

She blushed, but did not refuse it. The same evening she rushed to the Count's apartment in a state of the greatest excitement. "I am beside myself," she stammered; "I have been most deeply insulted."

"By whom?" the Count asked excitedly.

"By your friend, who has dared to send me some jewelry to-day. I suppose he looks upon me as a lost woman; perhaps I am already looked upon as belonging to the *demi-monde,* and this I owe to you, to you alone, and to my mad love for you, to which I have sacrificed my honor and everything. Everything!" She threw herself down and sobbed, and would not be pacified until the Count gave her his word of honor that he would set aside every consideration for his friend, and obtain satisfaction for her at any price. He met the Italian the same evening at a card party and questioned him.

"I did not, in the first place, send the lady the jewelry, but I gave it to her myself, not, however, until she had asked me to do so."

"That is a shameful lie!" the Count shouted furiously. Unfortunately, there were others present. His friend took the matter seriously, and the next morning sent his seconds to the Count.

Some of their real friends tried to settle the matter in another way, but his bad angel, the Viennese, who required thirty thousand florins, drove the Count to his death. He was found in the Prater with his friend's bullet in his chest. A letter in his pocket spoke of suicide, but the police did not doubt for a moment that a duel had taken place. Suspicion soon fell on the Italian, but when they went to arrest him he had already made his escape.

The broken-hearted father of the man who had been killed in the duel had hastened to Vienna on receipt of a telegram, and a few hours after his arrival the husband of the beautiful enigmatical woman called on him and demanded money: "My wife was your son's most intimate friend," he stammered, in embarrassment, in order to justify his action as well as he could. "Oh! I know that," the old Count replied, "and female friends of that kind want to be paid immediately, and in full. Here are the thirty thousand florins."

And our Goldkind? She paid her debts, and then withdrew from the scene for a while. She had been compromised, certainly, but then she had risen in value in the eyes of a certain class of men who can only adore and sacrifice themselves for a woman when her foot is on the threshold of vice and crime.

I saw her last during the Franco-German war, in the beautiful Mirabell Garden, at Salzburg. She did not appear to feel any qualms of conscience, for she had become considerably stouter, which made her more attractive, more beautiful, and consequently more dangerous, than she was before.

The Ill-omened Groom

AN Austrian banker discovered one day that a serious robbery had occurred in his home. Jewels, a valuable watch set with diamonds, his wife's miniature in a frame set with brilliants, and a considerable sum in money, the whole amounting in value to a hundred and fifteen thousand florins, had been stolen from his room. He went to the Director of Police to give notice of the robbery, but at the same time begged as a special favor that the investigation might be carried on as quietly and considerately as possible, as he declared that he had not the slightest ground for suspecting anybody in particular, and did not wish any innocent person to be accused.

"First of all, give me the names of all the persons who regularly go into your bedroom," the Police Director said.

"Nobody except my wife, my children, and Joseph, my valet; a man for whom I would answer as I would for myself.''

"Then you think him absolutely incapable of committing such a deed?"

"Most decidedly I do," the banker emphatically replied.

"Very well; then can you remember whether on the day on which you first missed the articles that have been stolen or on any days immediately preceding it anybody who was not a member of your household happened by chance to go to your bedroom?"

The banker thought for a moment and then said, with some hesitation:

"Nobody, absolutely nobody."

The experienced official, however, was struck by the banker's slight embarrassment and momentary blush, so he took his hand, and, looking him straight in the face, he said:

"You are not quite candid with me; somebody was with you, and you wish to conceal the fact from me. You must tell me everything."

"No, no; indeed, there was no one here."

"Then at present there is only one person on whom any suspicion can rest—and that is your valet."

"I will vouch for his honesty," the banker replied immediately.

"You may be mistaken, and I shall be obliged to question the man."

"May I beg you to do it with every possible consideration?"

"You may rely upon me for that."

An hour later the banker's valet was in the Police Director's private room. The official first of all looked at his man very closely, and then came to the conclusion that such an honest, unembarrassed face and such quiet, steady eyes could not possibly belong to a criminal.

"Do you know why I have sent for you?"

"No, your honor."

"A serious theft has been committed in your master's house," the Police Director continued, "in his bedroom. Do you suspect anybody? Who has been in the room within the last few days?"

"Nobody but myself, except my master's family."

"Do you not see, my good fellow, that by saying that you throw suspicion on yourself?"

"Surely, sir," the valet exclaimed, "you do not believe . . ."

"I must not believe anything; my duty is merely to investigate and to follow up any traces that I may discover," was the reply. "If you have been the only person to go into the room within the last few days I must hold you responsible."

"My master knows me . . ."

The Police Director shrugged his shoulders. "Your master has vouched for your honesty, but that is not enough for me. You are the only person on whom, at present, any suspicion rests, and therefore I must—sorry as I am to do so—have you arrested."

"If that is so," the man said, after some hesitation, "I prefer to speak the truth, for my good name is more to me than my situation. Somebody was in my master's apartments yesterday."

"And this somebody was . . ."

"A lady."

"A lady of his acquaintance?"

The valet did not reply for some time.

"It must come out," he said at length. "My master has met a woman—you understand, sir, a pretty, fair woman; and he seems to be very fond of her, and goes to see her, but secretly, of course, for if my mistress were to find it out there would be a terrible scene. This person was in the house yesterday."

"Were they alone?"

"I showed her in myself, and she was in the bedroom. I had to call my master at once, as his confidential clerk wanted to speak to him, and so she was in the room alone for about a quarter of an hour."

"What is her name?"

"Cecilia K——; she is a Hungarian." At the same time the valet gave him her address.

Then the Director of Police sent for the banker, who, on being brought face to face with his valet, was obliged to acknowledge the truth of the facts which the latter had alleged, painful as it was for him to do so; whereupon orders were given to take Cecilia K—— into custody.

In less than half an hour, however, the police officer who had been despatched for that purpose returned and said that she had left her apartments, and most likely the capital also, the previous evening. The unfortunate banker was almost in despair. Not only had he been robbed of a hundred and fifty thousand florins, but at the same time he had lost the beautiful woman. He could not grasp the idea that a woman whom he had surrounded with Asiatic luxury, whose strangest whims he had gratified, and whose tyranny he had borne so patiently, could have deceived him so shamefully, and now he had a quarrel with his wife and an end of all domestic peace into the bargain.

The only thing the police could do was to send detectives after the lady, who had denounced herself by her flight, but it was all of no use. In vain did the banker, in whose heart hatred and thirst for revenge had taken the place of love, implore the director of police to employ every means to bring the beautiful criminal to justice, and in vain did he undertake to be responsible for all the costs of her prosecution, no matter how heavy they might be. Special police officers were told off to try and discover her, but Cecilia K—— was so inconsiderate as not to allow herself to be caught.

Three years had passed and the unpleasant story appeared to have been forgotten. The banker had obtained his wife's pardon, and the police did not appear to trouble themselves about the beautiful Hungarian any more.

The scene now changes to London. A wealthy lady who created much sensation in society, and who made many conquests both by her beauty and her behavior, was in need of a groom. Among the many applicants for the situation was a young man whose good looks and manners gave people the impression that he must have been very well educated. This was a recommendation in the eyes of the lady's maid, and she took him immediately to her mistress's boudoir. When he entered he saw a beautiful, voluptuous-looking woman, twenty-five years of age at most, with large, bright eyes and blue-black hair, which seemed to increase the brilliancy of her fair complexion. She was lying on a sofa. She looked at the young man, who had thick black hair, and who turned his glowing black eyes to the ground, beneath her searching gaze, with evident satisfaction, and she seemed particularly taken with his slender, athletic build, and said half lazily and half proudly:

"What is your name?"

"Lajos Mariassi."

"A Hungarian?"

A strange look came into her eyes.

"Yes."

"How did you come here?"

"I am one of the many emigrants who have forfeited their country and their life; and I, who come of a good family, and who was an officer of the Honveds must now . . . go into service, and thank God if I find a mistress who is at the same time beautiful and an aristocrat, as you are."

Mademoiselle Zoë—that was the lovely woman's name—smiled, and at the same time showed two rows of pearly teeth.

"I like your appearance," she said, "and I feel inclined to take you into my service, if you are satisfied with my terms."

"A lady's whim," her maid said to herself, when she noticed the looks which Mademoiselle Zoë gave her manservant, "which will soon pass away." But that experienced female was mistaken that time.

Zoë was really in love, and the respect with which Lajos treated her put her into a very bad temper. One evening, when she intended to go to the Italian Opera, she countermanded her carriage and refused to see her noble admirer, who was ready to throw himself at her feet, and she ordered her groom to be sent up to her.

"Lajos," she began. "I am not at all satisfied with you."

"Why, Madame?"

"I do not wish to have you about me any longer; here are your wages for three months. Leave the house immediately." And she began to walk up and down the room impatiently.

"I will obey you, Madame," the groom replied, "but I shall not take my wages."

"Why not?" she asked hastily.

"Because then I should be under your authority for three months," Lajos said, "and I intend to be free, this very moment, so that I may be able to tell you that I entered your service, not for the sake of your money, but because I love and adore you as a beautiful woman."

"You love me!" Zoë exclaimed. "Why did you not tell me sooner? I merely wished to banish you from my presence, because I love you and did not think that you loved me. But you shall smart for having tormented me so. Come to my feet immediately."

The groom knelt before the lovely girl, and from that moment Lajos became her favorite. Of course he was not allowed to be jealous, as the young lord was still her official lover, who had the pleasure of paying her bills, and besides him, there was a whole army of so-called "good friends," who were fortunate enough to obtain a smile now and then, and who, in return, had permission to present her with rare flowers, a parrot, or diamonds.

The more intimate Zoë became with Lajos the more uncomfortable she felt when he looked at her, as he frequently did, with undisguised contempt. She was wholly under his influence and was afraid of him, and one day, while he was playing with her dark curls, he said jeeringly:

"It is usually said that contrasts attract each other, and yet you are as dark as I am."

She smiled and then tore off her black curls, and immediately the most charming, fair-haired woman was sitting by the side of Lajos, who looked at her attentively, but without any surprise.

He left the house at about midnight in order to look after the horses, as he said, and she retired. In two hours' time she was roused from her slumbers and saw a police inspector and two constables by the side of her bed.

"Whom do you want?" she cried.

"Cecilia K——"

"I am Mademoiselle Zoë."

"Oh! I know you," the inspector said, with a smile; "be kind enough to take off your dark locks, and you will be Cecilia K——. I arrest you in the name of the law."

"Good heavens!" she stammered. "Lajos has betrayed me."

"You are mistaken, Madame," the inspector replied; "he has merely done his duty."

"What? Lajos . . . my adorer?"

"No, Lajos, the detective."

Cecilia got out of bed, and the next moment sank fainting to the floor.

In His Sweetheart's Livery

AT the time the talented young Hungarian poet first made her acquaintance and discovered her histrionic ability, in 1847, she was a beautiful girl though not of high moral character. She is now an intellectual, elegant, great lady and a celebrated actress.

The slim, intense girl, with her bright brown hair and her large blue eyes, attracted the careless poet, and he loved her, and all that was good and noble in her nature blossomed forth in the sunshine of his poetic adoration.

They lived in an attic in the old imperial city on the Danube, and she shared his poverty, his triumphs, and his pleasures, and would have become his true and faithful wife if the Hungarian revolution had not torn him from her arms.

The poet became the soldier of freedom and followed the Magyar tricolor and the Honved drums, while she was carried away by the current of the movement in the capital, and might have been seen discharging her musket, like a brave Amazon, at the Croats, who were defending the town against Görgey's attacking battalions.

But at last Hungary was subdued, and was governed as if it had been a conquered country.

It was said that the young poet had fallen at Temesvar, and the girl wept for him, and then married another man, which was nothing either new or extraordinary. Her name was now Frau von Kubinyi, but her married life was not happy; and one day it occurred to her that the poet had told her that she had a talent for the stage, and whatever he said had always proved correct, so she separated from her husband, studied a few parts, appeared on the stage, and the public, the critics, actors, and magazine writers were at her feet.

She obtained a very profitable engagement, and her reputation increased with every part she played; and before the end of a year after her first appearance she was the lioness of society. Everybody paid homage to her, and the wealthiest men tried to obtain her favor; but she remained cold and reserved until the general commanding the district, a handsome man of noble bearing and a gentleman in the highest sense of the word, approached her.

Whether she was flattered at seeing that great man, before whom millions trembled and who had to decide over the life and death, the honor and happiness of so many thousands, enslaved by her soft curls, or whether her enigmatical heart for once really felt what true love was, suffice it to say that in a short time the General was under her command and was surrounding her with the luxury of an Eastern queen.

But just then a miracle occurred—the resurrection of a dead man. Frau von Kubinyi was driving through the Corso in the General's carriage; she was lying back negligently in the soft cushions and looking carelessly at the crowd on the pavement. Suddenly she caught sight of a common Austrian soldier and screamed aloud.

Nobody heard that cry which came from the depths of a woman's heart; nobody saw how pale and how excited was that woman who usually seemed made of marble, not even the soldier who was the cause of her agitation. He was a Hungarian poet who, like so many other Honveds, now wore the uniform of an Austrian soldier.

Two days later, to his no small surprise, he was told to report to the general in command, as orderly, and when he presented himself he told him to go to Frau von Kubinyi's and to await her orders.

Our poet only knew her by report, but he hated and despised most cordially the beautiful woman whom report associated with the enemy of his country. He had no choice, however, but to obey.

When he arrived at her house he seemed to be expected, for the porter knew his name, took him into his lodge, and without any further explanation told him immediately to put on the livery of his mistress, which was lying there ready for him. He ground his teeth but resigned himself without a word to his wretched, though laughable, fate; it was quite clear that the actress had some purpose in making the poet wear her livery. He tried to remember whether he could formerly have offended her by his notices as a theatrical critic, but before he could arrive at any conclusion he was told to go and show himself to Frau von Kubinyi.

She evidently wished to enjoy his humiliation.

He was shown into a small drawing-room, which was furnished with an amount of taste and magnificence such as he had never seen before, and was told to wait. But he had not been alone many minutes before the door curtains were parted and Frau von Kubinyi came in, calm but deadly pale, in a splendid robe of some Turkish material, and he recognized his former sweetheart.

"Irma!" he exclaimed.

The cry came from his heart, and it affected the woman who was surfeited with pleasure so greatly that the next moment her head was on the shoulder of the man whom she had believed to be dead. But only for a moment, and then he freed himself from her.

"We are fated to meet again thus!" she began.

"Not through any fault of mine," he replied bitterly.

"And not through mine, either," she said quickly; "everybody thought that you were dead, and I wept for you; that is my justification."

"You are really too kind," he replied sarcastically. "How can you condescend to make any excuses to me? I wear your livery, and you have to order and I obey; our relative positions are clear enough."

Frau von Kubinyi turned away to hide her tears.

"I did not intend to hurt your feelings," he continued; "but I must confess that it would have been better for both of us if we had not met again. But what do you mean by making me wear your livery? Is it not enough that I have been robbed of my happiness? Does it afford you any pleasure to humiliate me as well?"

"How can you think that?" the actress exclaimed. "Ever since I discovered your unhappy lot I have thought of nothing but the means of delivering you from it, and until I succeed in doing this I can at least make it more bearable for you."

"I understand," the unhappy poet said, with a sneer. "And in order to do this you have begged your present worshiper to turn me into a footman."

"What a thing to say to me!"

"Can you find any other pleasure as a substitute? You wish to punish me for having loved you, idolized you, I suppose?" the poet continued. "So exactly like a woman! But I can perfectly well understand that the situation promises to have a fresh charm for you. . . ."

Before he could finish what he was saying the actress quickly left the room; he could hear her sobbing, but he did not regret his words, and his contempt and hatred for her only increased, when he saw the extravagance and the princely luxury with which she was surrounded. But what was the use of his indignation? He was wearing her livery and he was obliged to wait upon her and to obey her, for she had the corporals at her command, and it really seemed as if he incurred the vengeance of the offended woman, as if she wished to make him feel her whole power, as if he were not to be spared the deepest humiliation.

The General and three of Frau von Kubinyi's friends, who were also on the stage—one a ballet dancer and the two other actresses—had come to tea, and he was to wait on them.

While tea was being prepared he heard them laughing in the next room and the blood rushed to his head. When the butler opened the door Frau von Kubinyi appeared on the General's arm; she did not, however, look at her new footman, her former lover, triumphantly or contemptuously, but she gave him a glance of the deepest commiseration.

Could he, after all, have wronged her in his thoughts?

Hatred and love, contempt and jealousy were struggling in his breast, and when he had to fill the glasses the bottle shook in his hand.

"Is this the man?" the General said, looking at him closely.

Frau von Kubinyi nodded.

"He was evidently not born for a footman," the General added.

"And still less for a soldier," the actress observed.

These words fell heavily on the unfortunate poet's heart, but she was evidently taking his part and trying to rescue him from his terrible position.

Suspicion, however, once more gained the day.

"She is tired of all pleasure and satiated with enjoyment," he said to himself; "she requires excitement and it amuses her to see the man whom she formerly loved, and who, as she knows, still loves her, tremble before her. And when she pleases she can see me tremble; not for my life but for fear of the disgrace which she can inflict upon me at any moment if it should give her any pleasure."

But suddenly the actress gave him a look which was so sad and so imploring that he looked down in confusion.

From that time he remained in her house without performing any duties and without receiving any orders from her; in fact, he never saw her and did not venture to ask after her, and two months had passed in this way when the General unexpectedly sent for him. He waited, with many others, in the anteroom, and when the General came back from parade he saw him and beckoned him to follow him, and as soon as they were alone he said:

"You are free, as you have been allowed to purchase your discharge."

"Good heavens!" the poet stammered, "how am I to——"

"That is already done," the General replied. "You are free."

"How is it possible? How can I thank your excellency?"

"You owe me no thanks," he replied; "Frau von Kubinyi bought your release."

The poor poet's heart seemed to stop; he could not speak nor even stammer a word, but with a low bow he rushed out and tore wildly through the streets until he reached the mansion of the woman whom he had so misunderstood, quite out of breath; he must see her again and throw himself at her feet.

"Where are you going to?" the porter asked him.

"To Frau von Kubinyi's."

"She is not here."

"Not here?"

"She has gone away."

"Gone away? Where to?"

"She started for Paris two hours ago."

The Jennet

THE day after General Daumont de Croisailles held a review he was sure to receive a package of notes from women.

Some were scribbled on paper with a love emblem at the top, as if from some sentimental milliner; others were ardent, as if saturated with curry.

Among them were some which evidently came from a woman of the world, who was tired of her monotonous life, had lost her head, and let her pen run on, without exactly knowing what she was writing, with those mistakes in spelling here and there which seemed to indicate the disordered beating of her heart.

The General certainly looked magnificent on horseback. There was something of the fighter, something bold and defiant about him, a valiant look, as our grandmothers used to say, when they threw themselves into the arms of the conquerors, in the intervals of a campaign, though these same conquerors had loud, rough voices, even when they were making love, from being obliged to raise them above the noise of the firing, and used violent gestures, as if they were swinging their swords and issuing orders, and they did not waste time over useless refinements and in squandering the precious hours, which were counted so avariciously, in minor caresses.

As soon as he appeared sitting erect in the saddle, sword in hand, preceded by dragoons and a little ahead of his staff, amid the clatter of hoofs and jingling of scabbards and bridles and the waving plumes and uniforms glittering in the sun, his cocked hat with the black plumes slightly tilted to one side, the surging crowd cheered him as if he had been some popular minister, whose arrival had been announced beforehand.

That tumult of strident voices that resounded from one end of the great square to the other, and was prolonged like the sound of the rising tide beating against the shore; that rattle of rifles, and the sound of the music that alternated with blasts of the trumpets all along the line, made the General's heart swell with unspeakable pride.

He posed in spite of himself, and thought of nothing but ostentation and adulation. He continually touched his horse with the spur and worried it, so as to make it appear restive, and to prance and rear, to champ its bit, and to cover itself with foam; and then he would continue his inspection, galloping from regiment to regiment with a satisfied smile, while the good old infantry captains, sitting on their thin Arab horses, their toes well turned out, said to one another:

"I should not like to have to ride a confounded restive brute like that!"

But the General's aide-de-camp, litle Jacques de Montboron, could easily have reassured them, for he knew those famous thoroughbreds, as he had had to break them in, and had received a thousand trifling instructions about them.

They were generally more or less spavined brutes which he had bought at auction for a nominal sum, and so quiet and well in hand that they might have been held with a silk thread, but they were well made, with bright eyes and coats that glistened like satin. They seemed to know their part, and stepped out, pranced and reared, and made way for themselves, as if they had just come out of the riding-school at Saumur.

That was his daily task, his obligatory service.

He broke them in, one after the other, and transformed them into veritable mechanical horses, accustomed them to bear the noise of trumpets and drums, and of musketry, without starting, tired them out by long rides the evening before every review, and bit his lips to prevent himself from laughing when people declared that General Daumont de Croisailles was a splendid horseman, who really loved danger.

A horseman! That was almost as true as history! But the aide-de-camp discreetly kept up the illusion, outdid the others in flattery, and related unheard-of feats of the General's horsemanship.

And, after all, breaking in horses was not more irksome than carrying on a monotonous and dull correspondence about the buttons on the gaiters, or than thinking over projects of mobilization, or than going through accounts in which he lost himself as in a labyrinth. It was not in vain that, from the very first day that he entered the military academy at Saint-Cyr, he had learned that sentence which begins the rules of the Department of the Interior:

"As discipline constitutes the principal strength of an army, it is very important for every superior to obtain absolute respect and instant obedience from his inferiors."

He never rebelled, but accustomed himself to become a sort of Monsieur Loyal, spoke to his chief in the most obsequious manner, and counted on being promoted over the heads of his fellow officers.

General Daumont de Croisailles was not married and did not intend to disturb the tranquillity of his bachelor life as long as he lived, for he loved all women, whether they were dark, fair, or red-haired, too devotedly to love only one, who would grow old and worry him with useless complaints.

He was gallant, as men used to be called in the good old days; he kissed the hands of those women who refused him their lips, and as he did not wish to compromise his dignity and be the talk of the town, he had rented a small house just outside it.

It was close to the canal in a quiet street with courtyards and shady gardens, and as nothing is less amusing than the racket of jealous husbands or the brawling of excited women who are disputing or raising their voices in lamentation, and as it is always necessary to foresee some unfortunate incident or other, some unlucky mishap, some absurdly imprudent action, some forgotten love appointment, the house had five different doors.

So discreet that he reassured even the most

timid, and certainly not given to melancholy, he understood extremely well how to vary his kisses and his ways of proceeding; how to work on women's feelings, and to overcome their scruples, to obtain a hold over them through their curiosity to learn something new, by the temptation of a comfortable, well-furnished, warm room, fragrant with flowers, where a little supper was awaiting them.

Men mistrusted that ancient Lovelace as if he had been the plague, when they had sketched out some charming adventure for themselves; for he always managed to discover their secret and outgeneral them.

To some women he held out the irresistible argument that led astray Danaë, that of gold; others were attracted by his uniform and military rank, and their pride was flattered at the thought of seeing him at their feet.

His pay, allowances, and his private income of fifteen thousand francs, all went in this way, like water that leaks from a cracked bottle.

He was continually on the alert and looked out for intrigues with the acuteness of a detective, followed women about and had all the impudence and cleverness of the fast man who has made love for forty years without ever meaning anything serious, who knows all its lies, tricks, and illusions, and who can still do a march without halting on the road or requiring too much music to put him in proper trim. And in spite of his age and gray hairs, he could have given a sub-lieutenant points, and was very often loved for his own sake, which is the dream of men who have passed forty and do not intend to give up the game just yet.

There were a dozen or more women whom he

had not captivated, however, and one of these was Jacques de Montboron's sweetheart. She was a little marvel, that Madame Courtade, whom the Captain had met in an ecclesiastical warehouse in the Faubourg Saint-Exupère, and she was not yet twenty. They had begun by smiling at each other, and by exchanging those long looks when they met which seemed to ask for charity.

Montboron used to pass in front of the shop at the same hours, and stop for a moment with the appearance of a lounger who was loitering about the streets, but presently her supple figure would appear, pink and fair, shedding the brightness of youth and almost childhood around her, while her looks showed that she was delighted at the gallant incident which dispelled the monotony and weariness of her life for a time, and gave rise to vague but delightful hopes.

Was love, that love which she had so constantly invoked, really knocking at her door at last, and taking pity on her unhappy isolation? Did that officer whom she met whenever she went out, when coming out of church, or when out for a walk in the evening—as if he had been watching for her—who said so many delightful things to her with his fascinating eyes, really love her as she wished to be loved, or was he merely amusing himself at that game, because he had nothing better to do in their quiet little town?

But in a short time he wrote to her and she replied to him, and at last they managed to meet in secret, to make appointments, and to talk together.

She knew all the cunning tricks of a simple girl, who has tasted the most delicious of sweets with the tip of her tongue, and acting in concert, and giving each other the word, so that there might be no awkward mistake, they managed to make the husband their unwitting accomplice, without his having the least idea of what was going on.

Courtade was an excellent fellow, who saw no further than the tip of his nose, incapable of rebelling, flabby, fat, steeped in devotion, and thinking too much about heaven to see what a plot was being hatched against him in our unhappy vale of tears, as the Psalmist calls it.

In the good old days of confederacies, he would have made an excellent chief of a corporation; he loved his wife more as a father than a husband, believing that at his age a man ought no longer to think of such trifles, and that, after all, the only real happiness in life was to keep a good table and to have a good digestion; and so he ate like four canons, and drank in proportion.

Only once during his whole life had he shown anything like energy—but he used to relate that occurrence with all the pride of a conqueror recalling his most heroic battle—and that was on the evening when he refused to allow the bishop to take his cook away, quite regardless of any of the consequences of such a daring deed.

In a few weeks the Captain became his regular table companion and his best friend. He had begun by telling Courtade in a boastful manner that, in order to keep a vow that he had made to St. George during the charge up the slope at Yron, during the battle of Gravelotte, he wished to send two censers and a sanctuary lamp to his village church.

Courtade did his utmost, and all the more readily as this unexpected customer did not appear to pay any regard to money. He sent for several goldsmiths, and showed Montboron models of all kinds; the latter hesitated, however, and did not seem able to make up his mind, and discussed the subject, designed ornaments himself, gained time, and thus managed to spend several hours every day in the shop.

In fact, he was quite at home in the place, shook hands with Courtade, called him " my dear fellow," and did not wince when Courtade took his arm familiarly before other people and introduced him to his customers as, " My excellent friend, the Marquis de Montboron." He could go in and out of the house as he pleased, whether the husband was at home or not.

The censers and the lamp were sent in due course to Montboron's château at Pacy-sur-Romanche (in Normandy), and when the package was undone it caused the greatest surprise to Jacques's mother, who was more accustomed to receiving requests for money from her son than ecclesiastical objects.

Suddenly, however, without rhyme or reason, little Madame Courtade became insupportable and enigmatical. Her husband could not understand it at all, and grew uneasy and continually consulted his friend, the captain.

Etiennette's character seemed to have completely changed; she found fifty pretexts for deserting the shop, for coming in late, for avoiding *tête-à-têtes,* in which people come to explanations and mutually become irritated, though such matters usually end in a reconciliation, amid a torrent of kisses.

She disappeared for days at a time, and soon Montboron, who was not fitted to play the part of a Sganarelle, either by age or temperament, became convinced that his lady-love was making a fool of him, that she was flirting with the General, and as he was as jealous as an Andalusian, and felt a horror of that kind of pleasantry, he swore that he would make his rival pay a hundredfold for the trick which he had played him.

The Fourteenth of July was approaching, when there was to be a grand parade of the whole garrison on the large parade ground; and all along the paling which shut off the spectators from the soldiers itinerant dealers had put up their stalls, and there were mountebanks' and clairvoyants' booths, menageries, and a large circus, which had gone through the town in caravans, with a great noise of trumpets and of drums.

The General had given his aide-de-camp instructions beforehand, for he was more anxious than ever to surprise people, and to have a horse like an equestrian model, an animal which should outdo that famous black horse of General Boulanger's, about which the Parisian loungers had talked so much, and he told Montboron not to mind what the price was, as long as he found him a suitable steed.

When the Captain, a few days before the review, brought him a chestnut jennet with a long tail and flowing mane, which would not keep quiet for five seconds, but kept on shaking its head, had unusual action, answered the slightest touch of the leg, and stepped out as if it knew no other motion, General Daumont de Croisailles showered compliments upon him, and assured him that he knew few officers who possessed his intelligence and his value, and that he should not forget him when the time came to recommend him for promotion.

Not a muscle of the Marquis de Montboron's face

moved, and when the day of the review arrived, he was at his post on the staff that followed the General, who sat as upright as a dart in the saddle, and looked at the crowd to see whether he could not recognize some old or new female acquaintance, while his horse pranced and plunged.

He rode on to the review ground, amid the increasing noise of applause, with a smile upon his lips, when, suddenly, at the moment that he galloped up into the large square formed by the troops drawn up in a line, the band of the fifty-third regiment struck up a quick march, and, as if obeying a preconcerted signal, the jennet began to turn round, and to accelerate its speed, in spite of the furious tugs at the bridle which the rider gave.

The horse performed beautifully, followed the rhythm of the music, and appeared to be acting under some invisible impulse, and the General had such a comical look on his face, he looked so disconcerted, rolled his eyes, and seemed to be the prey to such terrible exasperation, that he might have been taken for some character in a pantomine, while his staff followed him without being able to comprehend this new whim of his.

The soldiers presented arms, the music continued, though the performers were much astonished at this interminable ride.

The General at last became out of breath, and could scarcely keep in the saddle, and the women, in the crowded ranks of the spectators, gave prolonged, nervous laughs, which made the old *roué's* ears tingle with annoyance.

The horse did not stop until the music ceased, and then it knelt down with bent head and put its nose to the ground.

It nearly gave General de Croisailles an attack of the jaundice, especially when he found out that it was his aide-de-camp's tit for tat, and that the horse came from a circus which was giving performances in the town. And what irritated him all the more was that he could not even set it down against Montboron and have him sent to some terrible out-of-the-way hole, for the Captain sent in his resignation, wisely considering that sooner or later he should have to pay the cost of that little trick, and that the chances were that he should not get any further promotion, but remain stationary, like a cab which some swindler leaves standing for hours at one end of an arcade, while he makes his escape at the other end.

Kind Girls

EVERY Friday regularly about eleven o'clock in the morning he came into the courtyard, laid his soft felt hat at his feet, struck a few chords on his guitar, and then began to sing a ballad in a full, rich voice. And presently, at every window in the four sides of that dull, barrack-like building, some girls appeared, one in an elegant dressing-gown, another in a little jacket, most of them with their breasts and arms bare, all of them just out of bed, with their hair hastily twisted up, their eyes blinking in the sudden blaze of sunlight, their complexions dull, and their eyes still heavy from want of sleep.

They swayed themselves backward and forward to his slow melody, and gave themselves up to the enjoyment of it, and coppers and even silver poured into the handsome singer's hat, and more than one of them would have been glad to follow the penny which she threw to him, and to go away with the singer who had the voice of a siren, and who seemed to say to all these amorous girls: "Come, come to my retreat, where you will find a palace of crystal and gold, and wreaths which are always fresh, and happiness and love which never die."

That was what they seemed to hear, those unhappy girls, when they heard him sing the song of the old legends which they had formerly believed. That was what they understood by the foolish words of the ballad. That and nothing else, for how could any one doubt it on seeing the fresh roses on their cheeks and the tender flame which flickered like a mystic night light in their eyes, which had, for the moment, become the eyes of innocent young girls again? But of young girls who had grown up very quickly, alas! who were very precocious, and who very soon became the women that they were, poor vendors of love, always in search of love for which they were paid.

That was why, when he had finished his second ballad, and sometimes even sooner, languorous looks appeared in their eyes. The boatman of their dreams, the water sprite of fairy tales, vanished in the mist of their childish recollections, and the singer reassumed his real shape, that of musician and strolling player, whom they wished to pay to be their lover. And the coppers and small silver were showered on him again, with engaging smiles, with the leers of a street-walker, even with "*p'st, p'st,*" which soon transformed the barrack-like courtyard into an enormous cage full of twittering birds, while some of them could not restrain themselves, but said aloud, rolling their eyes with desire: "How handsome the creature is! Good heavens, how handsome he is!"

He was really handsome, and nobody could deny it, and even too handsome, with a regular beauty which almost palled on people. He had large, almond-shaped, gentle eyes, a Grecian nose, a bow-shaped mouth, hidden by a heavy mustache, and long, black, curly hair; in short, a head fit to be put into a hairdresser's window, or, better still, perhaps, upon the front page of the ballads which he was singing. But what made him still handsomer was that his self-conceit had a look of sovereign indifference, for he was not satisfied with not replying to the smiles, the ogles, and the *p'st, p'st's,* by taking no notice of them; but when he had finished he shrugged his shoulders, he winked mischievously, and turned up his lips contemptuously, which said very clearly: "The stove is not being heated for you, my little kittens!"

Often one might have thought that he expressly wished to show his contempt, and that he tried to make himself thought unpoetical in the eyes of all those amorous girls, and to check their love, for he cleared his throat ostentatiously and offensively, more than was necessary, after singing, as if he would have liked to spit at them. But all that did not make him unpoetical in their eyes, and many of them, who were absolutely mad on him, went so far as to say that "he did it like a swell!"

The girl who in her enthusiasm had been the first to utter that exclamation of intense passion, and who, after throwing him small silver, had thrown him a twenty-franc gold piece, at last made up her mind to have an explanation. Instead of a *p'st, p'st,* she spoke to him boldly one morning, in the presence of all the others, who religiously held their tongues.

"Come up here," she called out to him, and from habit she added: "I will be very nice, you handsome dark fellow."

At first they were dumfounded at her audacity, and then all their cheeks flushed with jealousy, and the flame of mad desire shot from their eyes. From every window there came a perfect torrent of:

"Yes, come up, come up." "Don't go to her! Come to me."

And, meanwhile, there was a shower of halfpence, of francs, of gold coins, as well as of cigars and oranges, while lace pocket-handkerchiefs, silk neckties, and scarfs fluttered in the air and fell round the singer like a flight of many-colored butterflies.

He picked up the spoil calmly, almost carelessly, stuffed the money into his pocket, made a bundle of the furbelows, which he tied up as if they had been soiled linen, and then, raising himself up and putting his felt hat on his head, he said:

"Thank you, ladies, but indeed I cannot."

They thought that he did not know how to satisfy so many demands at once, and one of them said: "Let him choose."

"Yes, yes, that is it!" they all exclaimed unanimously.

But he repeated: "I tell you I cannot."

They thought he was excusing himself out of gallantry, and several of them exclaimed, almost with tears of emotion: "Women are all heart!" And the same voice that had spoken before (it was one of the girls who wished to settle the matter amicably) said: "We must draw lots."

"Yes, yes, that is it," they all cried. And again there was a religious silence, more religious than before, for it was caused by anxiety, and the beat ings of their hearts may have been heard.

The singer profited by it, to say slowly: " cannot have that, either; nor all of you at once, no one after the other; nothing! I tell you that I can not."

"Why? Why?" And now they were almos screaming, for they were angry and sorry at th same time. Their cheeks had gone from scarlet t livid, their eyes flashed fire, and some shook thei fists menacingly.

"Silence!" the girl cried who had spoken first "Be quiet, you pack of huzzies! Let him explai himself, and tell us why!"

"Yes, yes, let us be quiet! Make him explai himself, in God's name!"

Then, in the fierce silence that ensued, the singe said, opening his arms wide, with a gesture of de spairing inability to do what they wanted:

"What do you want? It is very amusing, bu I cannot do more. I have two girls of my own al ready at home."

Mamma Stirling

TALL, slim, her figure well defined under her transparent dress of gauze, which fell in straight folds, with gold bracelets on her slender wrists, with languor in her rich voice, and something undulating and feline in the rhythmical swing of her wrist and hips, Tatia Caroly was singing one of those sweet Creole songs which call up some far distant fairyland and unknown caresses, for which the lips remain always thirsting.

Footit, the clown, was leaning against the piano. His blackened face, and his mouth that looked like the red gash from a saber cut, and his wide-open eyes, all expressed feelings of the most extravagant emotion, while some negroes squatted on the ground and accompanied the orchestra by strumming on some yellow, hollow gourds.

But what made the women and children laugh

most in the pantomime of the "New Circus" was the incessant quarrel between an enormous Danish hound and a poor supernumerary, who was blackened like a negro minstrel and dressed like a mulatto woman. The dog was always annoying him, following him, and snapping at his legs and at his old wig with his sharp teeth, and he tore his coat and his silk pocket-handkerchief whenever he could get hold of it. The man would positively allow himself to be molested and bitten, playing his part with dull resignation, with the mechanical unconsciousness of a man who has come down in the world, and who gains his livelihood as best he can, and who has already endured worse things than that.

Half turning round to the two clubmen with whom she had just been dining at the Café Anglais, as she handled her large fan of black feathers with a pretty, supple motion of her wrist, while the light fell on to the nape of her fair neck, Noële de Fréjus exclaimed: "Wherever did they unearth that horrible, grotesque figure?"

Lord Shelley, who was a pillar of the circus, and who knew the performances, the length of time the acrobats had been performing, and the private history of all of them, whether clowns or circus riders, replied: "Do not you recognize him, my dear?"

"That lump of soot? Are you joking?"

"He certainly has changed very much, poor fellow, and not for the better. James Stirling was, however, once a model of manly beauty and elegance, and he led such an extravagant life that all sorts of stories were rife about him, and many people declared that he was some high-class adventurer. . . . At any rate, he thought no more of danger than he did of smoking a good cigar.

"Do you not remember him at the Hippodrome, when he stood on the bare back of a horse and drove five others tandem at full gallop and without making a mistake, but checking them or urging them on with his thin, muscular hands, just as he pleased? And he seemed to be riveted to the horse, as if he had been held on by invisible hands."

"Yes, I remember him . . . James Stirling," she said. "The circus rider, James Stirling, on whose account that tall girl, Caro, who was also a circus rider, gave that old stager, Blanche Taupin, a cut right and left across the face with her riding whip, because she had tried to get him from her. . . . But what can have happened to bring him down to such a position?"

Horrible, hairy monkeys, grimacing under their red and blue masks, had invaded the arena, and with their hair hanging down on their bare shoulders, looking very funny with their long tails, their gray skin tights and their velvet breeches, these female dancers twisted, jumped, hopped, and drew their lascivious and voluptuous circle more closely round Chocolat, who shook the red skirts of his coat, rolled his eyes, and showed his large white teeth in a foolish smile, as if he were the prey to irresistible desire, and yet terribly afraid of what might happen; and Lord Shelley, helping himself to some grapes out of a basket that Noële de Fréjus offered him, said: "It is not a very cheerful story, but then true stories rarely are. At the time when he was still unknown, and when he used to have to tighten his belt more frequently for lack of enough to eat and drink, James Stirling followed the destinies of a circus which traveled with its vans from fair to fair and from place to place, and fell in love with a gypsy columbine, who also formed part of this wandering, half-starved company.

"She was not twenty and astonished the others by her rash boldness, her absolute contempt for danger and obstacles, and her strange and adroit strength. She charmed them also by a magic attraction which came from her hair, which was darker than a starless night, from her large, black, coaxing, velvety eyes, that were concealed by the fringe of such long lashes that they curled upward, from her scented skin, that was as velvety as rice-paper, and every touch of which was a suggestive and tempting caress, from her firm, full, smiling, childlike mouth, which uttered nothing but laughter, jokes, and love songs, and seemed made for kissing.

"She rode barebacked horses without bit or bridle, stretched herself at full length on their backs as if on a bed, her flowing hair mingling with their manes, swaying her supple body to their most impetuous movements, at other times standing almost on their shoulders or on the croup, while she juggled with looking-glasses, brass balls, knives that flashed as they twirled rapidly round in the smoky light of the paraffin lamps that were fastened to the tent poles.

"Her name was Sacha, that pretty Slavonic name which has such a sweet and strange sound, and she loved him entirely, because he was handsome, strong, and spoke to women very gently, as one talks to quite little children who are easily frightened and made to cry, and it was on her account that in a quarrel in Holland he knocked down an Italian wild beast tamer, with a blow between the two eyes.

"They adored each other so that they never thought of their poverty, but were just as devoted when they had nothing to eat, not even an unripe apple stolen from an orchard nor a lump of bread which they had begged on the road of some charitable soul. And they were often obliged to stop for the night in the open country, and shiver in the old, badly-closed vans, and had to be very sparing with the wood, and could not light up the snow with those large bivouac fires, whose smoke rises in such fantastic, spiral curls, and whose flames look like a spot of blood at a distance, seen through the mist.

"It was one of those bohemian, quasi-matrimonial arrangements which are often more enduring than ours, and in which a man and a woman do not part for a mere caprice, a dream, or a piece of folly.

"By-and-by she was no longer good for anything, and had to give up appearing on the program, for she was *enceinte.* James Stirling worked for both, and thought that he should die of grief when, after three days of intense suffering, she died with her hand in his.

"And now, all alone, crushed by grief, so ill that at times he thought his heart had stopped, the circus rider lived for the child which the dead woman had left him as a legacy. He bought a goat so that it might have pure milk, and brought it up with such infinite, deep, womanly tenderness that the child called him 'Mamma,' and in the circus they nicknamed him 'Mamma Stirling.'

"The boy was like his mother, and one might have said that he had brought James luck, for he had made his mark, was receiving a good income, and appeared in every performance. Well-made and agile, and profiting by the lessons which he received at the circus, little Stirling was soon fit to appear on the posters, and the night when he made his first appearance at Franconi's old Tom Pears, the clown, who understood such matters better than most, exclaimed:

"'My boy, you will make your way if you don't break your neck first!'

"'I will take care of that, Monsieur Pears,' the lad replied, with a careless shrug of his shoulders.

"He was extremely daring, and when he threw himself from one trapeze to the other, in a bold flight through the air, one might almost have fancied in the silvery electric light that he was some fabulous bird with folded wings, and he executed all his feats with unequaled natural grace, without seeming to make an effort, but he unbraced his limbs of steel and condensed all his strength in one supreme, mad leap. His chest, under its pearl-gray tights, hardly rose, and there was not a drop of perspiration on his forehead among the light curls which framed it like a golden halo.

"He had an almost disdainful manner of smiling at the public, as if he were an artist who loves his profession and who is amused at danger, rather than an acrobat who is paid to amuse people after dinner, and during his most difficult feats he often uttered a shrill cry like that of some wild beast which defies the sportsman as it falls on its prey. But that sportsman is always on the alert, and he is the Invisible, which closes the brightest eyes and the most youthful lips forever. In spite of one's self, one was excited by it and could have wished, from a superstitious instinct, that he would not continually give that defiant cry, which seemed to give him pleasure.

"James Stirling watched over him as the mother

of an actress does who knows that she is in some corner and fears dangerous connections in which the strongest are entangled and ruined; and they lived together in a boarding-house near the Arc de Triomphe. It was a very simple apartment, with immense posters of every color and in every language, on which the name of Stirling appeared in large, striking letters, pinned to the wall; photographs with inscriptions, and tinsel wreaths, though there were two of real laurel, that were covered with dust and were gradually falling to pieces.

"One night the young fellow for the first time did not come home, and returned only in time for rehearsal, tired, with blue rims under his eyes, his lips cracked and feverish, and with pale cheeks, but with such a look of happiness and such a peculiar light in his eyes that Mamma Stirling felt as if he had been stabbed, and had not the strength to find fault with him; and, emboldened, radiant, longing to give vent to the mad joy which filled his whole being, to express his sensations and recount his happiness, like a lad talking to his elder brother, he told James Stirling his love intrigue from beginning to end, and how much in love he was with the fair-haired girl who had clasped him in her arms and told him she loved him.

"It had been coming for some time, he said. She went to every performance, and always occupied the same box. She used to send him letters by the usher, letters which smelled like bunches of violets, and she always smiled at him when he came into the ring to bow to the public, amid the applause and recalls; and it was that smile, those red, half-opened lips, which seemed made for kisses and tender words, that attracted him like some strange, fragrant fruit. Sometimes she came with gentlemen in evening dress and with gardenias in their button-holes, who seemed to bore her terribly, if not to disgust her. And he was happy, although he had never yet spoken to her, that she had not that smile for them which she had for him, and that she appeared dull and sad, like somebody who is homesick or who has a great longing for something.

"On other evenings she would be all alone, with black pearls in the lobes of her small ears that were like pink shells, and would get up and leave her box as soon as he had finished his performance on the trapeze . . . while the evening before she had carried him off almost forcibly in her carriage, without even giving him time to get rid of his tights and the india-rubber armlets that he wore on his wrists. Oh! that return in the cold, in the semi-obscurity, through which the trembling light of the street lamps shone, that warm clasp of her arms round him which imprisoned him and by degrees drew him close to that warm body whose slightest throb and shiver he felt, as if she had been clothed in impalpable gauze, and which intoxicated him.

"And those despotic, imperious, divine kisses, when she pressed her lips to his, as if to make him dream of an eternity of bliss, intoxicating, overwhelming him with delight! And the carriage rolled on at a quick trot, through the silence of the snow, and they did not even hear the noise of the wheels, which buried themselves in that white carpet as if it had been cotton-wool. Suddenly, however, they began talking at random, like people who are not quite themselves and who have uncorked too many bottles of champagne on a benefit night.

"She questioned him and laughed at his theatrical slang, wrapped her otter-skin rug round his legs, and murmured: 'Come close to me, darling; at any rate, you are not cold, I hope?'

"When they reached her pretty little house, with old tapestry and delicate-colored plush hangings, they found supper waiting for them, and she amused herself by waiting on him herself with the manners of a saucy waitress. And then there were kisses, constant, insatiable, maddening kisses, and the lad exclaimed, with glistening eyes, at the thoughts of future meetings: 'If you only knew how pretty she is! And then it is nicer than anything else in the world to obey her, to do whatever she wants, and to allow one's self to be loved as she wishes!'

"Mamma Stirling was very uneasy, but resigned himself to the inevitable, and, seeing how infatuated the boy was, he took care not to be too sharp with him or to keep too tight a hand upon the reins. The woman who had entangled the lad was a fast woman, and nothing else, and, after all, the old stager preferred that to one of those excitable women of the world, who are as dangerous for a man as the plague, whereas a girl of that sort can be taken and given up again, and one does not risk one's heart at the same time as one does one's skin, for a man knows what they are worth. He was mistaken, however. Nelly d'Argine—she is married to a Yankee now and has gone to New York with him—was one of those vicious women whom a man can only wish his worst enemy to have, and she had merely taken a fancy to the young fellow because she was bored to death, and because her senses were roused like smoldering embers which come to life again when a fire is nearly out.

"Unfortunately, the boy had taken the matter

seriously, and was very jealous, and as suspicious as a deer, and never imagined that this love affair could come to an end; and, proud as he was, with his hot gypsy blood, he wished to be the only lover, the only master, who could not be shown the door, like a troublesome and importunate parasite.

"Stirling had saved some money by dint of a hard struggle and had invested it in the Funds against a rainy day, when he should be too old to work and to gain a livelihood, and when he saw how madly in love his son was and how obstinate in his lamentable folly he gave him all his savings and deprived himself of his stout and gin so that the boy might have money to give away and might continue to be happy and not have any cares, and so between them they supported Nelly.

"Stirling's debts accumulated, and he mortgaged his salary for years in advance to the usurers who haunt circuses as if they were gambling hells, who are on the watch for passions, poverty, and disappointments, who keep plenty of ready-stamped bill paper in their pockets, as well as money, which they haggle over coin by coin. But in spite of all this the lad sang, did his turn, and amused himself, and would say, as he kissed his father on both cheeks: How kind you are in spite of everything!'

"After a month he became too exacting; he followed her, questioned her, and worried her with perpetual scenes, and Nelly found that she had had enough of her gymnast; he was a toy which she had done with and worn out, and which was now only in her way and only fit to throw into the gutter. She was satiated with him, and became once more the tranquil woman whom nothing can move and who baits her traps quite calmly in order to find a husband and make a fresh start. And so she turned the young fellow out of doors as if he had been some beggar soliciting alms. He did not complain, however, and did not say anything to Mamma Stirling, but worked as he had done in the past and mastered himself with superhuman energy, so as to hide the grief that was gnawing at his heart and killing him, and the disenchantment with everything that was making him sick of life.

" Some time afterward, when there was to be a special performance for the officers, seeing Nelly d'Argine there in a box surrounded by her usual admirers, appearing indifferent to everything that was going on and not even apparently noticing that he was performing and was being heartily applauded, he threw his trapeze forward as far as he could, at the end of the performance, and, exerting all his strength and certain that he should fall beyond the protecting net, he flung himself furiously into space.

" A cry of horror resounded from one end of the house to the other when he was picked up disfigured and with nearly every bone in his body broken. The unfortunate young fellow was no longer breathing, his chest was crushed in and blood-stained froth was issuing from his lips, and Nelly d'Argine made haste to leave the house with her friends, saying, in a tone of annoyance:

" 'It is very disgusting to come in the hopes of being amused and to witness an accident!'

" And Mamma Stirling, who was ruined and in utter despair, and who cared for nothing more in this world, after that took to drinking, would get constantly drunk, and rolled from public house to public house and bar to bar, and as the worst glass of vitriol still cost two sous he became reduced to undertaking the part which you have seen, to dabble in the water, to blacken himself, and to allow himself to be bitten.

"Ah! What a wretched thing life is for those who are kind and who have too much heart!"

The Marquis

WHEN that obstinate little Sonia, with the Russian name and Russian caprices, said: "I choose to do it," it was quite useless to remonstrate. She was so delicate and pretty, with her slightly tilted nose and her rosy, childish cheeks, and every female perversity was reflected in the depths of her strange eyes, which were the color of the sea on a stormy evening. Yes, she was very charming, very fantastic, and, above all, so Russian, so deliciously and imperiously Russian, and all the more Russian as she came from Montmartre, and in spite of this, not one of her seven admirers who composed her usual menagerie had laughed when their enslaver said one day:

"You know my feudal castle at Pludun-Herlouët, near Saint-Jacut-de-la-Mer, which I bought two years ago, and in which I have not yet set foot? Very well, then! The day after to-morrow, which is the first of May, we will have a housewarming there."

The seven had not asked for any further explanation, but had accompanied little Sonia, and were now ready to sit down to dinner under her presidency in the dining-room of the old castle, which was situated ten hours from Paris. They had arrived there that morning; they were going to have dinner and supper together, and start off again at daybreak next morning; such were Sonia's orders, and nobody had made the slightest objection.

Two of her admirers, however, who were not yet used to her sudden whims, had felt some surprise, which was quickly checked by expressions of enthusiastic pleasure on the part of the others.

"What a delightfully original idea! Nobody else would have thought of such things! Positively, nobody else. Oh, these Russians!" But those who had known her for some time, and who had been consequently prepared not to be surprised at anything, found it all quite natural.

It was half-past six in the evening, and the gentlemen were going to dress. Sonia had made up her mind to keep on her morning gown, or if she dressed she would do so later. Just then she was not inclined to move out of her great rocking-chair from which she could see the sun setting over the sea. The sight always delighted her very much. It might have been taken for a large red billiard ball, rebounding from the green cloth. How curious it was! And how lucky that she was all alone to look at it, for those seven would not have understood it at all! Those men never have any soul, have they?

Certainly the sunset was strange at first, but at length it made her sad, and just now Sonia's heart felt almost heavy, though the very sadness was sweet. She was congratulating herself more than ever on being alone, so as to enjoy that languor which was almost like a gentle dream; when, in perfect harmony with that melancholy and sweet sensation, a voice rose from the road, which was overhung by a terrace, a tremulous but fresh and pure voice singing the following words to a slow melody:

"Walking in Paris,
  Having my drink,
A friend of mine whispered:
  What do you think?
If love makes you thirsty,
Then wine makes you lusty."

The sound died away, as the singer continued on his way, and Sonia was afraid that she should not hear the rest; it was really terrible; so she jumped out of the rocking-chair, ran to the balustrade of the terrace, and, leaning over it, called out: "Sing it again! I insist on it. The song, the whole song!"

On hearing this, the singer looked round and then came back, without hurrying, however, and as if he were prompted by curiosity rather than by any desire to comply with her order. Holding his hand over his eyes, he looked at Sonia attentively, and on her part, she had plenty of time to look closely at him.

He was an old man of about sixty-five, and his rags and the wallet over his shoulder denoted a beggar, but Sonia immediately noticed that there was a certain amount of affectation in his wretchedness.

His hair and beard were not shaggy and ragged, as such men usually wear it, and he evidently had his hair cut occasionally, and had a fine, and even distinguished, face, as Sonia said to herself. But she did not pay much attention to that, as for some time she had noticed that old men at the seaside nearly all looked like gentlemen.

When he got to the foot of the terrace the beggar stopped, and shook his head and said: "Pretty! The little woman is very pretty!" But he did not obey Sonia's order, and she repeated it, almost angrily this time, beating a violent tattoo on the stonework. "The song, the whole song!"

He did not seem to hear, but stood there gaping, with a vacant smile on his face, his head rather inclined toward his left shoulder, a thin stream of saliva trickling from his lips on to his beard, and his looks becoming more and more ardent: "How stupid I am!" Sonia suddenly thought. "Of course he is waiting for something." She felt in her pocket, in which she always carried some gold by way of change, took out a twenty-franc piece, and threw it down to the old man. He, however, did not take any notice of it, but continued looking at her ecstatically, and was only roused from his state of bliss by receiving a handful of gravel which she threw at him, right in his face.

" Do sing! " she exclaimed. " You must, I will have it; I have paid you." And then, still smiling, he picked up the napoleon and threw it back on to the terrace, and said proudly, though in a very gentle voice: " I do not ask for charity, little lady; but if it gives you pleasure, I will sing you the whole song, the whole of it, as often as you please." And he began the song again, in his tremulous voice, which was more tremulous than it had been before, as if he were much affected.

Sonia was overcome, and without knowing why was moved to tears; delighted because the man had spoken to her so familiarly, and rather ashamed at having treated him as a beggar. Her whole being was carried away by the slow rhythm of the melody, which related an old love story, and when he had finished he again looked at her with a smile, and as she was crying he said to her: " I daresay you have a beautiful horse, or a little dog that you are very fond of, which is ill? Take me to it, and I will cure it; I understand it thoroughly. I will do it for nothing, because you are so pretty."

She could not help laughing. " You must not laugh," he said. " What are you laughing at? Because I am poor? But I am not, for I had work yesterday, and again to-day. I have a bag full. See, look here! " And from his belt he drew a leather purse in which coppers rattled. He poured them out into the palm of his hand, and said merrily: " You see, little one, I have a purse. Forty-seven sous; forty-seven! "

" So you won't take my napoleon? " Sonia said.

"Certainly not," he replied. "I do not wan it; and then, I tell you again, I will not accep alms. So you do not know me?"

"No, I do not."

"Very well, ask any one in the neighborhood Everybody will tell you that the Marquis does no live on charity."

The Marquis! At that name she suddenly re membered that two years ago she had heard hi story. It was at the time that she bought the prop erty, and the vendor had mentioned the Marqui as one of the curiosities of the soil. He was sai to be half silly, at any rate an original, almost i his dotage, living by any lucky bits that he coul make as horse trader and veterinary. The peasant gave him a little work, as they feared that he migh throw spells over any one who refused to emplo him. They also respected him on account of hi former wealth and of his title, for he had been rich very rich, and they said that he really was a Mar quis, and it was said that he had ruined himself i Paris by speculating. The reason, of course, wa women!

At that moment the dinner bell began to ring and a wild idea entered Sonia's head. She ran t the little door that opened on to the terrace, over took the musician, and with a ceremonious bow sh said: "Will you do me the pleasure and the hono of dining with me, Marquis?"

The old man left off smiling and grew serious he put his hand to his forehead, as if to brin old recollections back, and then, with a very forma old-fashioned bow, he said:

"With pleasure, my dear." And, letting hi wallet drop, he offered Sonia his arm.

When she introduced this new guest to her admirers, all the seven, even the best drilled, started. "I see what disturbs you," she said. "It is his dress. Well! It really leaves much to be desired. But wait a moment, that can soon be arranged."

She rang for her lady's maid, and whispered something to her, and then she said: "Marquis, your bath is ready in your dressing-room. If you will follow Sabina she will show you to it. These gentlemen and I will wait dinner for you."

As soon as he had gone out she said to the youngest there: "And now, Ernest, go upstairs and undress; I will allow you to dine in your morning-coat, and you will give your dress-coat and the rest to Sabina for the Marquis."

Ernest was delighted at having to play a part in the piece, and the six others clapped their hands. "Nobody else would have thought of such a thing; nobody, nobody!"

Half an hour later they were sitting at dinner, the Marquis in a dress-coat on Sonia's left, and it was a great disillusion for the seven. They had reckoned on having some fun with him, and Ernest especially, who set up as a wit, had intended to draw him out. But at the first attempt of this sort Sonia had given him a look which they all understood, and dinner began very ceremoniously for the seven, but merrily and without restraint between Sonia and the old man.

They pulled very long faces, those seven, but inwardly, if one can say so, for, of course, they could not dream of showing how put out they were, and those inward long faces grew longer still, when Sonia said to the old fellow, quite suddenly: "I say, how stupid these gentlemen are! Suppose we leave them to themselves?"

The Marquis rose, offered her his arm again, and said: "Where shall we go?" But Sonia's only reply was to sing the couplet of a song which she remembered.

And the seven, who were altogether dumfounded this time, and who could not conceal their vexation, saw the couple disappear out of the door which led to Sonia's apartments. "Hum!" Ernest ventured to say, "this is really rather too much!" "Yes," the eldest of the menagerie replied. "It certainly is rather peculiar, but it will do! You know there is nobody like her for thinking of such things!"

The next morning the château bell woke them up at six o'clock, when they agreed to return to Paris, and the seven men asked each other whether they should go and wish Sonia good morning, as usual, before she was out of her room. Ernest hesitated more than any of them about it, and it was not until Sabina, her maid, came and told them that her mistress insisted upon it that they could make up their minds to do so, and they were surprised to find Sonia in bed.

"Well!" Ernest asked boldly, "and what about the Marquis?"

"He left very early," Sonia replied.

"A queer sort of Marquis, I must say!" Ernest observed contemptuously, and growing bolder.

"Why, I should like to know?" Sonia replied, drawing herself up. "The man has his own habits, I suppose!"

"Do you know, Madame," Sabina observed, "that he came back half an hour after he left?"

"Ah!" Sonia said, getting up and walking about the room. "He came back? What did he want, I wonder?"

"He did not say, Madame. He merely went upstairs to see you. He was dressed in his old clothes again."

And suddenly Sonia uttered a loud cry, and clapped her hands, and the seven came round to see what had caused her emotion.

"Look here! Just look here!" she cried. "Do look on the mantelpiece! It is really charming! Do look!"

And with a smiling and yet somewhat melancholy expression in her eyes, with a tender look which they could not understand, she showed them a small bunch of wild flowers, by the side of a heap of pennies.

Mechanically she took them up and counted them, and then began to cry.

There were forty-seven of them.

The Mountebanks

THE clever manager of the Eden Réunis Theater, as the critics called him, was counting on a great success, and had invested his last franc in the affair, without thinking of the morrow or of the bad luck which had been pursuing him so inexorably for months past. For a whole week the walls, the kiosks, shop windows, and even the trees, had been placarded with flaming posters, and from one end of Paris to the other carriages were to be seen covered with fancy sketches by Chéret, representing two strong, well built men who looked like ancient athletes. The younger of them, who was standing with his arms folded, had the vacant smile of an itinerant mountebank on his face, and the other, who was dressed in what was supposed to be the costume of a Mexican trapper, held a revolver in his hand. There were large type advertisements in all the papers, that the Montefiores would appear without fail at the Eden Réunis the next Monday.

Nothing else was talked about, for the puff and humbug attracted people. The Montefiores, like fashionable toys, succeeded that whimsical jade Rose Péché, who had gone off the preceding autumn, between the third and fourth acts of the burlesque *Ousca Iscar,* in order to make a study of love in the company of a young fellow of seventeen, who had just entered the university. The novelty and danger of their performance revived and agitated the curiosity of the public, for there seemed to be an implied threat of death, or, at any rate, of wounds and of blood in it, and it seemed as if they defied danger with absolute indifference. And that always pleases women; it holds them and masters them, and they grow pale with emotion and cruel enjoyment. Consequently, all the seats in the large theater were let almost immediately, and were soon taken for several days in advance. And stout Compardin, losing his glass of absinthe over a game of dominos, was in high spirits, and saw the future through rosy glasses, and exclaimed in a loud voice: "I think I have turned up trumps, by George!"

* * * * * * *

The Countess Regina de Villegby was lying on the sofa in her boudoir, languidly fanning herself. She had only received three or four intimate friends that day, Saint-Mars Montalvin, Tom Sheffield, and his cousin Madame de Rhouel, a Creole, who laughed as incessantly as a bird sings. It was growing dusk, and the distant rumbling of the carriages in the Champs-Elysées sounded like some somnolent rhythm. There was a delicate perfume of flowers; the lamps had not been brought in yet, and chatting and laughing they filled the room with a confused noise.

"Would you pour out the tea?" the Countess said suddenly, touching Saint-Mars's fingers with her fan. He was beginning a conversation in a low voice, and while he slowly filled the little china cup, he continued: "Are the Montefiores as good as the lying newspapers make out?"

Then Tom Sheffield and the others all joined in. They had never seen anything like it, they declared; it was most exciting, and made one shiver unpleasantly, as when the *espada* comes to close quarters with the infuriated brute at a bullfight.

Countess Regina listened in silence and nibbled the petals of a tea-rose.

"How I should like to see them!" giddy Madame de Rhouel exclaimed.

"Unfortunately, cousin," the Countess said, in the solemn tones of a preacher, "a respectable woman dare not let herself be seen in improper places."

They all agreed with her; nevertheless, Madame de Villegby was present at the Montefiores' performance two days later at the back of a stage box, dressed all in black, and wearing a thick veil.

And that woman, who was as cold as a steel buckler and who had married as soon as she left the convent in which she had been at school, without any affection or even liking for her husband, and whom the most skeptical respected as a saint, had a look of virgin purity on her calm face as she went down the steps of the Madeleine on Sundays, after high mass.

Countess Regina stretched herself nervously, grew pale, and vibrated like the strings of a violin on which an artist has been playing some wild symphony, and inhaled the nasty smell of the sawdust, as if it had been the perfume of a bouquet of unknown flowers, and clinched her hands, and gazed eagerly at the two mountebanks, whom the public applauded rapturously at every feat. And, contemptuously and haughtily, she compared those two men, who were as vigorous as wild animals that have grown up in the open air, with the rickety limbs that looked so awkward in the dress of the English huntsman who had tried to awaken her heart!

* * * * * * *

Count de Villegby had gone back to the country to prepare for his election as Councilor General, and the very evening that he started Regina again took the stage box at the Eden Réunis. Intoxicated as if by some love philter, she scribbled a few words on a piece of paper—the eternal formula that women write on such occasions:

"A carriage will be waiting for you at the stage door after the performance—An unknown woman who adores you."

And she gave it to an usher, who handed it to the Montefiore who was the champion pistol shot.

Oh! that interminable waiting in a malodorous cab, the overwhelming emotion, and the nausea of disgust, the fear, the desire of waking the coachman who was nodding on the box, of giving him her address, and telling him to drive her home. But she remained with her face against the window, mechanically looking at the dark passage, that was illuminated by a gas lamp, at the "actors' entrance," through which men were continually hurrying, talking in a loud voice, and chewing the end of a cigar which had gone out. She remained as if she were glued to the cushions, and tapped impatiently on the bottom of the cab with her heels.

When the actor, who thought it was a joke, made his appearance, she could hardly utter a word, for impure thoughts are as intoxicating as adulterated liquor. She raised her veil to show how young, beautiful, and desirable she was. He admired her and promised to meet her. But she soon wearied of him and began to flirt with his partner.

Through it all she maintained her serene expression which she wore on Sundays after mass.

The partner was very sentimental, and his head was full of romance. He thought the unknown woman, who merely used him as her plaything, really loved him, and he was not satisfied with clandestine meetings. He questioned her, besought her, and the Countess made fun of him. Then she flirted with each in turn. They did not know it, for she had forbidden them ever to talk about her to each other, under the penalty of never seeing her again, and one day the younger of them said with humble tenderness, as he knelt at her feet:

"How kind you are to love me and to want me! I thought that such happiness only existed in novels, and that ladies of rank only made fun of poor strolling mountebanks like us!"

Regina knitted her golden brows.

"Do not be angry," he continued, "because I followed you and found out where you lived, and your real name, and that you are a Countess, and rich, very rich."

" You fool! " she exclaimed, trembling with anger. " People can make you believe things as easily as they can a child! "

She had had enough of him; he knew her name and might compromise her. The Count might possibly come back from the country before the elections. She no longer had any feeling, any desire for those two admirers, whom a fillip from her rosy fingers could bend to her will. It was time to seek for fresh amusement elsewhere.

" Listen to me," she said to the champion shot, the next night, " I would rather not hide anything from you. I like your comrade very much better than I do you, and I do not want to have anything more to do with you."

" My comrade! " he repeated.

He uttered a furious cry and rushed at Regina with clinched fists. She thought he was going to strike her, and closed her eyes, but he had not the courage, so in despair and with bowed head he said hoarsely:

" Very well, we shall not meet again, since it is your wish."

The house at the Eden Réunis was full to overflowing. The violins were playing a soft and delightful waltz of Gungl's, which the reports of a revolver accentuated.

The Montefiores were standing opposite one another as in Chéret's picture, about a dozen yards apart, and an electric light was thrown on the younger, who was leaning against a large white target, while very slowly the other traced his outline with bullet after bullet. He aimed with prodigious skill, and the black dots on the cardboard marked the shape of his body. The applause drowned the orchestra and increased continually, when suddenly a shrill cry of horror resounded from one end of the hall to the other. The women fainted, the violins stopped, and the spectators jostled each other. At the ninth ball the younger brother had fallen to the ground an inert mass, with a gaping wound in his forehead. His brother did not move, and tl ere was a look of madness on his face, while the Countess de Villegby leaned on the ledge of her box and fanned herself calmly, as unmoved as any cruel goddess of ancient mythology.

The next day, between four and five, when she was surrounded by her usual friends in her little, warm Japanese drawing-room, it seemed strange to hear in what a languid and indifferent voice she exclaimed:

"They say that an accident happened to one of those famous clowns, the Monta . . . the Monti . . . what is his name, Tom?"

"The Montefiores, Madame!"

And then they began to talk about the sale by Angèle Velours, at the Hôtel Drouot, before she married Prince Storbeck. She was going to buy the former *Folies*.

A Night In Whitechapel

LEDANTEC and I were twenty-five, and we had come to London for the first time in our lives. It was a cold, foggy Saturday evening in December, and I think that is more than enough to explain why my friend and I were most abominably drunk, though, to tell the truth, we did not feel any discomfort from it. On the contrary, we were floating in an atmosphere of perfect bliss. We did not talk, certainly, for we were incapable of doing so, but then we had no inclination for conversation. What would be the good of it? We could so easily read all our thoughts in each other's eyes! And our thoughts consisted in the sweet and unique knowledge that we were thinking about nothing whatever.

It was not, however, in order to arrive at that state of delicious, intellectual inanity that we had gone to mysterious Whitechapel. We had gone into the first public house we saw, with the firm intention of studying manners and customs—not to mention morals—as spectators, artists, and philosophers; but in the second public house we entered we ourselves became like the objects of our investigations, that is to say, sponges soaked in alcohol. Between one public house and the other the outer air seemed to squeeze those sponges, which then got just as dry as before, and thus we rolled from public house to public house, until at last the sponges could not hold any more.

Consequently, we had for some time bidden farewell to our study of morals, and our outlook was more limited to two impressions: zigzagging through the darkness outside, and the gleam of light inside the public houses. As to the imbibing of brandies, whiskies, and gins, that was done mechanically, and our stomachs scarcely noticed it.

But what strange beings we had elbowed against during our long halts! What a number of faces to be remembered, what clothes, what attitudes, what talk, and what rags!

At first we tried to note them exactly in our memory, but there were so many of them, and our brain got muddled so quickly, that at present we had no very clear recollection of anything or anybody. Even objects that were immediately before us appeared to us in a vague, dusky phantasmagoria and became confounded with precious objects in an inextricable manner. The world became to us a sort of kaleidoscope, seen in a dream through the penumbra of an aquarium.

Suddenly we were aroused from this state of somnolence, awakened as if by a blow on the chest, and imperiously forced to fix our attention on what we saw, for amid this whirl of strange sights, one stranger than all attracted our eyes and seemed to say to us: "Look at me."

It was at the open door of a public house. A ray of light streamed into the street through the half-open door, and that brutal ray fell right on the specter that had just risen up there, dumb and motionless.

For it was indeed a specter, pitiful and terrible, and, above all, most real as it stood out boldly against the dark background of the street, which seemed still darker behind it!

Young, yes; the woman was certainly young; there could be no doubt about that, when one looked at her smooth skin, her smiling mouth which showed her white teeth, and her firm bust, which could be plainly noted under her thin dress.

But then how explain her perfectly white hair, not gray or growing gray, but absolutely white, as white as any octogenarian's?

And then her eyes, her eyes beneath her smooth brow, were surely the eyes of an old woman? Certainly they were, and of a woman one could not tell how old, for it must have taken years of trouble and sorrow, of tears and of sleepless nights, and a whole long existence, thus to dull, to wear out, and to spoil those glassy orbs.

Glassy? Not exactly that. For granulated glass still retains a dull and milky brightness, a recollection, as it were, of its former transparency. But her eyes seemed rather to have been made of metal which had turned rusty, and really if pewter could rust I should have compared them to pewter covered with rust. They had the dead color of pewter, and at the same time they emitted a glance which was the color of reddish water.

But it was not until some time later that I tried to define them thus approximately by retrospective analysis. At that moment, being altogether incapable of such an effort, I could only establish in my own mind the idea of extreme decrepitude and horrible old age which they produced in my imagination.

Have I said that they were set in very puffy eyelids, which had no lashes whatever, and on her forehead without wrinkles there was not a vestige of eyebrow? When I tell you this, and considering their dull look beneath the hair of an octogenarian, it is not surprising that Ledantec and I said in a low voice at the sight of this woman, who was evidently young:

"Oh! poor, poor old woman!"

Her great age was further accentuated by the terrible poverty that was revealed by her dress. If she had been better dressed, her youthful looks would, perhaps, have struck us more, but her thin shawl, which was all that she had over her chemise, her single petticoat, which was full of holes and almost in rags, and which did not nearly reach to her bare feet, her straw hat with ragged feathers and with ribbons of no particular color through age, it all seemed so ancient, so prodigiously antique!

From what remote, superannuated, abolished period did they all spring? One did not venture to guess, and by a perfectly natural association of ideas, one seemed to infer that the unfortunate creature herself was as old as her clothes were. Now, by *one* I mean Ledantec and myself; that is to say, two men who were abominably drunk, and who were arguing with the special logic of intoxication.

It was also under the softening influence of alcohol that we looked at the vague smile on those lips, revealing the teeth of a child, without stopping to reflect on the beauty of those youthful teeth, and seeing nothing except her fixed and almost idiotic smile, which no longer contrasted with the dull expression of her looks, but, on the contrary, accentuated it. For, in spite of her teeth, it was the smile of an old woman in our imagination, and as for me, I was really pleased at the thought of being so acute when I inferred that this grandmother with such pale lips had a set of teeth of a young girl, and still, thanks to the softening influence of alcohol, I was not angry with her for this artifice. I even thought it particularly praiseworthy, since, after all, the poor creature thus carried out her calling conscientiously, which was to seduce us. For there was no possible doubt about the matter, that this grandmother was nothing more nor less than a prostitute.

And then, drunk! Horribly drunk, much more drunk than Ledantec and I were, for we really could manage to say: "Oh! Pity the poor, poor old woman!" while she was incapable of articulating a single syllable, of making a gesture, or even of imparting a gleam of promise, a furtive flash of allurement to her eyes. With her hands crossed on her stomach, and leaning against the front of the public house, with her whole body as stiff as if she had been in a state of catalepsy, she had nothing alluring about her, except her sad smile, and that inspired us with all the more pity because she was even more drunk than we were; and so, by an identical, spontaneous movement, we each of us seized her by an arm, to take her into the public house with us.

To our great astonishment, she resisted, sprang back, and so was in the shadow again, out of the ray of light which came through the door, while at the same time she began to walk through the darkness and to drag us with her, for she was clinging to our arms. We followed her without speaking and without knowing where we were going, but without the least uneasiness on that score. Only, when she suddenly burst into violent sobs as she walked, Ledantec and I began to sob in unison.

The cold and the fog had suddenly congested our brains again, and we had again lost all precise consciousness of our acts, of our thoughts, and of our sensations. Our sobs had nothing of grief in them, but we were floating in an atmosphere of perfect bliss, and I can remember that at that moment it was no longer the exterior world which seemed to me as if I were looking at it through the penumbra of an aquarium; it was I myself, an *I* composed of three, which was changing into something that was floating adrift in something, though what it was I did not know, composed of palpable fog and intangible water, and it was exquisitely delightful.

From that moment I remember nothing more until what follows, which had the effect of a clap of thunder on me, and made me rise up from the bottom of the depth to which I had descended.

Ledantec was standing in front of me, his face convulsed with horror, his hair standing on end, and his eyes staring out of his head, as he shouted to me:

"Let us escape! Let us escape!" Whereupon I opened my eyes wide, and found myself lying on the floor in a room into which the daylight was shining. I saw some rags hanging against the wall, two chairs, a broken jug lying on the floor by my side, and in a corner a wretched bed, on which a woman was lying. She was doubtless dead, for her head was hanging over the side, and her long, white hair reached almost to my feet.

With a bound I was on my feet, like Ledantec.

"What!" I said to him, while my teeth chattered: "Did you kill her?"

"No, no," he replied. "But that makes no difference; let us be off."

I felt completely sober by this time, but I did think that he was still suffering somewhat from the effects of last night's drunk; otherwise, why should he wish to escape? Some remains of pity for the unfortunate woman forced me to say:

"What is the matter with her? If she is ill, we must look after her."

And I went to the wretched bed, in order to put her head back on the pillow, but I discovered that she was neither dead nor ill, but only sound asleep, and I also noticed that she was quite young.

She still wore that idiotic smile, but her teeth were her own and those of a girl. Her smooth skin and her firm bust showed that she was not more than sixteen, perhaps not so much.

"There! You see it, you can see it!" Ledantec said. "Let us be off."

He tried to drag me out, and he was still drunk; I could see it by his feverish movements, his trembling hands, and his nervous looks. Then he implored me, and said:

"I slept beside the old woman; but she is not old. Look at her; look at her; yes, she is old, after all!"

And he lifted up her long hair by handfuls; it was like handfuls of white silk, and then he added, evidently in a sort of delirium, which made me fear an attack of delirium tremens: "To think that I have begotten children, three, four children, who knows how many children, all in one night! And they were born immediately, and have grown up already! Let us be off."

Decidedly it was an attack of madness. Poor Ledantec! What could I do for him? I took his arm and tried to calm him, but he thought that I was going to try and make him go to bed with her again, and he pushed me away and exclaimed with tears in his voice: "If you do not believe me, look under the bed; the children are there; they are there, I tell you. Look here, just look here."

He threw himself down, flat on his stomach, and actually pulled out one, two, three, four children, who had hidden under the bed. I do not exactly know whether they were boys or girls, but all, like the sleeping woman, had white hair, the hair of an octogenarian.

Was I still drunk, like Ledantec, or was I mad? What was the meaning of this strange hallucination? I hesitated a moment, and shook myself to be sure that it was I.

No, no, I had all my wits about me, and I in reality saw that bunch of horrible little brats; they were all covering their faces with their hands, and were crying and squalling, and then, suddenly, one of them jumped on the bed; all the others followed his example, and the woman woke up.

And then we stood, while those five pairs of eyes, without eyebrows or eyelashes, eyes the dull color of pewter, with irises the color of red water, were steadily fixed on us.

"Let us be off! Let us be off!" Ledantec repeated, letting go of me, and this time I paid attention to what he said, and, after throwing some small change on the floor, I followed him, to make him understand, when he should be quite sober, that he saw before him a poor Albino prostitute, who had several brothers and sisters.

The Real One and the Other

"WELL, well," said Chasseval, as he stood with his back to the fire, "how could any of those respectable shopkeepers and winegrowers ever believe that that pretty little Parisian woman, with her soft, innocent eyes, like those of a Madonna, with such smiling lips and golden hair, who always dressed so simply, was not their candidate's wife?"

She was a wonderful help to him, and accompanied him even to the most outlying farms; went to the meetings in the small village cafés and had a pleasant and suitable word for every one, and did not recoil at a glass of mulled wine or a grip of the hand, and was always ready to join in a *farandole.* She seemed to be so in love with Elieane Rulhière, to trust him so entirely, to be so proud of forming half of his life, and of belonging to him, gave him such looks full of happiness and love, and listened to all he said so intently, that voters who might have hesitated allowed themselves by degrees to be talked over and persuaded, and promised their votes to the young doctor, whose name they had never heard mentioned in the district before.

That electoral campaign had been like a truant's escapade for Jane Dardenne; it was a delightful and unexpected holiday, and as she was an actress at heart, she played her part seriously, and threw herself into her character, and enjoyed herself more than she ever enjoyed herself in her most adventurous outings.

And then there came in the pleasure of being taken for a woman of good standing, of being flattered, respected, and envied, and of getting out of the usual groove for a time, and also the dream that at the end of this journey of a few weeks her lover would not separate from her on their return, but would sacrifice the woman whom he no longer loved, and whom he ironically used to call his Cinderella, to her.

At night, when they had laid aside all pretence, and were alone in their room in the hotel, she coaxed him and flattered him, spurred his ambition, threw her arms round him, and amid her kisses, whispered those words that are as wine to a man's heart.

Between them they captured the district and won the election easily; and in spite of his youth, Elieane Rulhière was elected by a majority of five thousand. Then, of course, there were more fêtes and banquets, at which Jane was present, and where she was received with enthusiastic shouts; there were fireworks, when she was obliged to set off the first rocket, and balls, at which she astonished those worthy people by her affability. And when they left, three little girls dressed in white, as if they were going to be confirmed, came on the platform and recited some complimentary verses to her while the band played the *Marseillaise* and the women waved their pocket-handkerchiefs and the men their hats, and as she leaned out of the carriage window, looking charming in her traveling costume, with a smile on her lips and with moist eyes, as was fitting at such a pathetic leavetaking, actress as she was, with a sudden and childlike gesture, she blew kisses to them from the tips of her fingers, and said:

"Good-by, my friends, good-by, only for the present; I shall never forget you!"

The Deputy, who was also very effusive, had invited his principal supporters to come and see him in Paris, as there were plenty of excursion trains. They all took him at his word, and Rulhière was obliged to invite them all to dinner.

In order to avoid any possible mishaps, he gave his wife a foretaste of their guests. He told her that they were rather noisy, talkative, and unpolished, and that they would, no doubt, astonish her by their manners and their accent, but that, as they had great influence and were excellent men, they deserved a good reception. It was a very useful precaution, for when they came into the drawing-room in their new clothes, expanding with pleasure, and with their hair pomatumed as if they had been going to a country wedding, they felt inclined to fall down before the new Madame Rulhière, to whom the Deputy introduced them, and who seemed to be perfectly at home there.

At first they were embarrassed, felt uncomfortable and out of place, did not know what to say, and had to seek for words; they buttoned and unbuttoned their gloves, answered her questions at random, and racked their brains to discover the solution of the enigma. Captain Mouredus looked at the fire with the fixed gaze of a somnambulist, Marius Barbaste scratched his fingers mechanically, while the three others, the factory manager, Casemajel, Roquetton, the lawyer, and Dustugue, the hotel proprietor, looked at Rulhière anxiously.

The lawyer was the first to recover himself. He got up from his armchair laughing heartily, dug the Deputy in the ribs with his elbow, and said:

"I understand it all, I understand it; you thought that people do not come to Paris to be bored, eh? Madame is delightful, and I congratulate you, Monsieur."

He gave a wink, and made signs behind his back to his friends, and then the captain had his turn.

"We are not boobies, and that fellow Roquetton is the most knowing of the lot of us. Ah! Monsieur Rulhière, without any exaggeration, you are the best of good fellows."

And, with a flushed face and expanding his chest, he said sonorously:

"They certainly turn them out very pretty in your part of the country, my little lady!"

Madame Rulhière, who did not know what to say, had gone up to her husband for protection; but she felt much inclined to go to her own room under some pretext or other, in order to escape from her intolerable task. She kept her ground, however, during the whole of dinner, which was a noisy, jovial meal, during which the five electors, with their elbows on the table and their waistcoats unbuttoned, and half drunk, told coarse stories and swore like troopers. But as the coffee and the liqueurs were served in the smoking-room, she took leave of her guests in an impatient voice, and went to her own room with the hasty step of an escaped prisoner who is afraid of being retaken.

The electors sat staring after her with gaping mouths, and Mouredus lit a cigar and said:

"Just listen to me, Monsieur Rulhière: it was very kind of you to invite us here to your little quiet establishment, but to speak to you frankly, I should not, in your place, wrong my lawful wife for such a stuck-up piece of goods as this one is."

"The captain is quite right," Roquetton, the notary, opined; "Madame Rulhière, the lawful Madame Rulhière, is much more amiable and altogether nicer. You are a scoundrel to deceive her; but when may we hope to see her?"

And with a paternal grimace he added:

"But do not be uneasy, we will all hold our tongue; it would be too sad if she were to find it out."

Charm of the Stable

THREE society women were sitting on a bench in the shade of some pine trees at Ischl, and were talking incidentally of their preference for all sorts of odors.

One of the ladies, Princess F——, a slim, handsome brunette, declared there was nothing like the smell of Russia leather. She wore dull-brown Russia leather boots, a Russia leather dress supporter, to keep her petticoats out of the dirt and dust, a Russia leather belt which spanned her wasplike waist, carried a Russia leather purse, and even wore a brooch and bracelet of gilt Russia leather. People declared that her bedroom was papered with Russia leather, and that her young gallants were obliged to wear high Russia leather boots and tight breeches, but that on the other hand, her husband was excused from wearing anything at all in Russia leather.

Countess H——, a very stout lady, who had formerly been very beautiful and of a very loving nature, after the fashion of her time, *à la* Parthenia and Griseldis, could not get over the vulgar taste of the young Princess. All she cared for was the smell of hay, and she it was who brought the scent new-mown hay into fashion. Her ideal was a freshly mown field in the moonlight, and when she rolled slowly along she seemed like a moving haystack and exhaled an odor of hay all about her.

The third lady's taste was even more peculiar than Countess H——'s, and more vulgar than the Princess's, for the small, delicate, light-haired Countess W—— lived only for—the smell of stables! Her friends could absolutely not understand this; the Princess raised her beautiful, full arm with its broad bracelet to her Grecian nose and inhaled the sweet smell of the Russia leather, while the sentimental hayrick exclaimed over and over again:

"How dreadful! What dost thou say to it, chaste moon?"

The delicate little Countess seemed very much embarrassed at the effect that her confession had had, and tried to justify her taste.

"Prince T—— told me that that smell had quite bewitched him once," she said; "it was in a Jewish town in Galicia, where he was quartered once with his hussar regiment, and a number of poor, ragged circus riders, with half-starved horses, came from Russia and put up a circus with a few poles and some rags of canvas, and the Prince went to see them, and found a woman among them who was neither young nor beautiful, but bold and impudent; and this woman wore a faded, bright red jacket trimmed with old, shabby imitation ermine, and that jacket stank of the stable, as the Prince expressed it, and she bewitched him with that odor, so that every time he saw her, and she smelt abominably of the stable, he felt as if he were magnetized."

"How disgusting!" both the other ladies said, and involuntarily held their noses.

"What dost thou say to it, chaste moon?" the haystack said with a sigh, and the little light-haired Countess was abashed, and held her tongue.

At the beginning of the winter season the three friends were together again in the gay imperial city on the blue Danube. One morning the Princess accidentally met the enthusiast of hay at the house of the little, light-haired Countess, and the two ladies were obliged to go after her to her private riding-school, where she was taking her daily lesson. As soon as she saw them she came up and beckoned her riding master to her to help her out of the saddle. He was a young man of extremely good and athletic build, which was set off by his tight breeches and his short velvet coat, and he ran up and took his lovely burden into his arms with visible pleasure to help her off the quiet, perfectly broken horse.

When the ladies looked at the handsome, vigorous man, it was quite enough to explain their little friend's predilection for the smell of a stable; but when the latter saw their looks she blushed up to the roots of her hair, and her only way out of the difficulty was to order the riding master, in a very authoritative manner, to take the horse back to the stable. He merely bowed with an indescribable smile, and obeyed her.

A few months afterward Viennese society was alarmed at the news that Countess W—— had been divorced from her husband. The event was all the more unexpected as they had apparently always lived very happily together, and nobody was able to mention any man on whom she had bestowed even the most passing attention, beyond the requirements of politeness.

Long afterward, however, a strange report became current. A chattering lady's maid declared that the handsome riding master had once so far forgotten himself as to strike the Countess with his riding whip; a groom had told the Count of the occurrence, and when he was going to call the insolent fellow to account for it the Countess placed herself before him, and thus gave occasion for the divorce.

Years had passed since then and the Countess H—— had grown stouter and more sentimental. Ischl and hayricks were not enough for her any longer; she spent the winter on lovely Lago Maggiore, where she walked among laurel bushes and cypress trees and was rowed about on the warm moonlight nights.

One evening she was returning home in the company of an English lady, who was also a great lover of nature, from Isola Bella, when they met a beautiful private boat in which a very unusual couple were sitting—a small, delicate, light-haired woman, wrapped in a white burnous, and a handsome, athletic man, in tight white breeches, a short black velvet coat trimmed with sable, a red fez on his head, and a riding whip in his hand.

Countess K—— involuntarily uttered a loud exclamation.

"What is the matter?" the English lady asked. "Do you know those people?"

"Certainly! She is a Viennese lady," Countess H—— whispered; "Countess W——"

"Oh! Indeed, you are quite mistaken; it is a Count Savelli and his wife. They are a handsome couple, don't you think so?"

When the boat came nearer she saw that it was indeed little Countess W——, and that the handsome man was her former riding master, whom she had married and for whom she had bought a Papal title; and as the two boats passed each other the short sable cloak, which was thrown carelessly over his shoulders, exhaled, like the old cat's-skin jacket of that impudent female circus rider, a strong odor of the stable.

Ugly

IN this blessed era of equality, mediocrity, of rectangular abomination, as Poe says, in this delightful age when every one tries to resemble every one else, so that it is impossible to distinguish the President of the Republic from a waiter; in these days, the forerunners of that future blissful time when everything in this world will be of a dull, neutral uniformity, in such an age one has the privilege, or, rather, it is one's duty, to be ugly.

He, however, assuredly exercised that privilege to the fullest extent, and he fulfilled that duty with the fiercest heroism, and to make matters worse, the mysterious irony of fate had caused him to be born with the name of Lebeau, while an ingenious godfather, the unconscious accomplice of the pranks of destiny, had given him the Christian name of Antinoüs.

Even among our contemporaries who were already on the high road to the coming ideal of universal ugliness, Antinoüs Lebeau was remarkable for his ugliness, and one might have said that he positively threw zeal, too much zeal, into the matter, though he was not hideous like Mirabeau, who made people exclaim: " Oh, the beautiful monster! "

Alas! No. He was without any beauty, even the beauty of ugliness. He was ugly, that was all, nothing more nor less; in short, he was uglily ugly. He was not humpbacked nor knock-kneed nor potbellied; his legs were not like a pair of tongs, and his arms were neither too long nor too short, and yet, there was an utter lack of uniformity about him, not only in painters' eyes, but also in everybody's, for nobody could meet him in the street without turning to look after him and thinking: " Good heavens! what an object! "

His hair was of no particular color, a light chestnut mixed with yellow. There was not much of it, but still he was not absolutely bald, though bald enough to allow his butter-colored pate to show. Butter-colored? Hardly! The color of margarine would be more applicable, and such pale margarine!

His face was also like margarine, but like adulterated margarine. By the side of it his cranium, the color of unadulterated margarine, looked almost like butter in comparison.

There was very little to say about his mouth! Less than little; the sum total was—nothing. It was a chimerical mouth.

But let us suppose that I have said nothing about him and replace this vain description by the useful formula: Impossible to describe. But you must not forget that Antinoüs Lebeau was ugly, that the fact impressed everybody as soon as they saw him, and that nobody remembered ever having seen an uglier person; and let us add that as the climax of his misfortune he knew it.

From this you will see that he was not a fool; neither was he of a bad disposition; but, of course, he was unhappy. An unhappy man thinks only of his wretchedness, and people take his nightcap for a fool's cap, while, on the other hand, goodness is only esteemed when it is cheerful. Consequently Antinoüs Lebeau passed for a fool, and an ill-tempered fool, and he was not even pitied because he was so ugly!

He had only one pleasure in life, and that was to go and roam about the darkest streets on dark nights and to hear some unfortunate creature say:

" Come with me, you handsome dark man! "

It was, alas! a furtive pleasure, and he knew that it was not true. For occasionally, when the woman was old or drunk and he profited by the invitation, as soon as they came under a street lamp they no longer murmured the fallacious *handsome dark man;* and when they saw him the old women grew still older, and the drunken women got sober. And more than one, although hardened against disgust and ready for all risks, said to him, and in spite of his liberal treatment:

" My little man, you are most confoundedly ugly, I must say."

At last, however, he renounced even that lamentable pleasure when he heard the still more lamentable words which a wretched woman could not help uttering when he accosted her:

" Well, he must be very hungry! "

Alas! He was a hungry, unhappy man; hungry for love, for something that should resemble love, were it ever so little; he longed not to love like a pariah any more, not to be exiled and proscribed in his ugliness. And the ugliest, the most repugnant woman would have appeared beautiful to him if she would only have consented not to think him ugly, or, at any rate, not to tell him so, and not to let him see that she felt horror at him on that account.

The consequence was that when he one day met a poor, blear-eyed creature with her face covered with scabs and bearing evident signs of alcoholism, with a driveling mouth and ragged and filthy skirts, to whom he gave liberal alms, for which she kissed his hand, he took her home with him, had her dressed in clean clothes, and taken care of, made her his servant and then his housekeeper. Next he raised her to his own position, and, finally, of course, he married her.

She was almost as ugly as he was! She really was; but only almost. Almost, but certainly not quite; for she was hideous, and her hideousness had its charm and its beauty, no doubt; that something by which a woman can attract a man. And she had proved that by deceiving him, and she let him see it better still by leading astray another man.

That other was actually uglier than Lebeau.

He was certainly uglier, that collection of every physical and moral ugliness, that companion of beggars whom she had picked up among her former vagrant associates, that jailbird, that vagabond covered with filth, with legs like a toad's, with a mouth like a lamprey, and a death's head in which the nose had been replaced by two holes.

"And you have wronged me with a wretch like that," the poor, deceived man said. "And why, why, you wretch? Why, seeing that he is uglier than I am?"

"Oh! no," she exclaimed. "You may say what you like, that I am a dirty low creature, but do not say that he is uglier than you are."

And the unhappy man stood there, vanquished and overcome by her last words, which she uttered without understanding all the horror which he would feel at them.

"Because, you see, he has his own particular ugliness, while you are merely ugly like everybody else is."

Under the Yoke

BEING of a simple and affectionate disposition, with quiet, regular habits and nothing to disturb the even tenor of his life, Monsieur de Loubancourt suffered at the loss of his wife more than is the case with most men. He regretted his lost happiness, blamed fate which separated united couples so brutally, and which chose a tranquil existence whose sleepy quietude had not hitherto been troubled by any cares or deceptions to rob it of its happiness.

Had he been younger he might perhaps have been tempted to start anew, to fill up the vacant place, and to marry again. But when a man is nearly sixty such ideas make people laugh, for they have something ridiculous and insane about them; and so he dragged on his dull and weary existence, escaped from all those familiar objects which constantly recalled the past to him, and went from hotel to hotel without taking an interest in anything, without becoming intimate with any one, even temporarily; inconsolable, silent, almost enigmatical, and looking funereal in his eternal black clothes.

He was generally alone, though on rare occasions he was accompanied by his only son, who used to yawn by stealth, and who seemed to be mentally counting the hours, as if he were performing some hateful, enforced duty.

Two years of this crystallization passed, and one was as monotonous and as void of incident as the other.

One evening, however, in a boarding house at Cannes, where he was staying on his wanderings, a young woman dressed in mourning was among the new arrivals, and sat next to him at dinner. She had a sad, pale face, that told of suffering, a beautiful figure, and large blue eyes with deep rings round them, but which, nevertheless, looked like the first stars which shine in the twilight.

All remarked her, and although he usually took no notice of women, no matter who they were, ugly or pretty, he looked at her and listened to her. He felt less lonely by her side, though he did not know why. He trembled with instinctive and confused happiness, just as if in some distant country he had found some female friend or relative who at last would understand him, tell him some news, and talk to him in his dear native tongue about everything that a man leaves behind him when he exiles himself from home.

What strange affinity had thrown them together thus? What secret forces had brought their grief in contact? What made him so sanguine and so calm, and incited him to take her suddenly into his confidence, and aroused his curiosity?

She was an experienced traveler, who had no illusions, and was in search of adventure; one of those women who have many aliases, and who, as they have made up their mind to swindle if luck is not on their side, act a continual part; an adventuress who could assume every accent; who to carry out her plans transformed herself into a Slav, into an American, or simply into a provincial; who was ready to take part in any comedy in order to make money and not be obliged to waste her strength and her brains on fruitless struggles or on wretched expedients. Thus she immediately guessed the state of this melancholy sexagenarian's mind and the illusions which attracted him to her, and scented the spoils which offered themselves to her cupidity without her seeking, and divined under what guise she ought to show herself, to make herself acceptable and loved.

She initiated him into depths of griefs unknown to him, by phrases cut short by sighs, by fragments of her story, which she finished with a despairing shrug of the shoulders and a sad smile, thus insensibly awakening his emotions. In a word, she triumphed over the last remaining doubts which might still have mingled with the affectionate pity with which that poor, solitary heart overflowed.

And so, for the first time since he had become a widower, the old man confided in another person, poured out his old heart into that soul which seemed to be so like his own, which seemed to offer him a refuge where he could be comforted, and where the wounds of his heart could be healed, and he longed to throw himself into those sisterly arms, to dry his tears, and to assuage his grief.

* * * * * * *

Monsieur de Loubancourt, who had married at twenty-five, as much for love as for reasons of prudence, had lived quietly and peacefully in the country, much more than in Paris. He was ignorant of the wiles of female tempters, and offered to creatures like Wanda Pulska, who was made up of lies and cared only for pleasure, a virgin soil on which any seed will grow.

She attached herself to him, became his shadow, and by degrees part of his life. She appeared to be a charitable woman who devoted herself to an unhappy man, who endeavored to console him, and who, in spite of her youth, was willing to be the inseparable companion of the old man in his slow daily walks. She never appeared to tire of his anecdotes and reminiscences, and she played cards with him. She waited on him carefully when he was confined to his room, appeared to be perfectly modest, and transformed herself; and, though she handled him skilfully, she seemed ingenuous and ignorant of evil. She acted like an innocent young girl who had just been confirmed; but for all that she chose dangerous hours and special places in which to be sentimental and to ask questions which agitated and disconcerted him, and she abandoned her slender fingers to his feverish hands, which pressed and held them in a tender clasp.

She gained such an influence over the old man that he one day made his will in her favor.

Informed, perhaps, by anonymous letters, or astonished because his father kept him altogether at a distance from him, and gave no signs of life, Monsieur de Loubancourt's son joined them in Provence. But Wanda Pulska, who had been preparing for that attack, waited for it fearlessly.

She was somewhat disturbed at that sudden visit, but was very charming and affable toward the newcomer, whom she reassured by her careless airs of a girl who took life as it came, and who was suffering from the consequences of a fault, but did not trouble her head about the future.

He envied his father, and grudged him such a treasure. Although he had come to combat her dangerous influence, and to treat the woman who had monopolized his father and who governed him as his sovereign as an enemy, he shrank from his task, lost his head, and thought of nothing but of supplanting the old man.

She managed him even more easily than she had managed Monsieur de Loubancourt, molded him just as she chose, made him her tool, without even giving him the tips of her fingers or granting him the slightest favor, induced him to commit so many imprudences that the old man grew jealous, watched them, discovered the intrigue, and found wild letters in which his son was angry, begged, threatened, and implored by turns.

One evening, when she knew that the old man had come in and was hiding in a dark cupboard in order to watch them, Wanda happened to be alone in the drawing-room, which was full of light, of beautiful flowers, with this young fellow of five-and-twenty. He threw himself at her feet and declared his love, and besought her to run away with him, and when she tried to bring him to reason and repulsed him, and told him in a loud and very distinct voice how she loved Monsieur de Loubancourt, he seized her wrists with brutal violence, maddened with passion, and stammered words of love.

"Let me go," she said; "let me go immediately.

You are a brute to take advantage of a woman like that. Please let me go, or I shall call the servants to my assistance."

The next moment the old man, terrible in his wrath, rushed out of his hiding place with clinched fists, his face distorted with rage, threw himself on the startled son, and, pointing to the door with a superb gesture, he said:

"You are a dirty scoundrel, sir. Get out of my house immediately, and never let me see you again!"

* * * * * * *

The comedy was over. Grateful for such fidelity and real affection, Monsieur de Loubancourt married Wanda Pulska, whose name appeared on the civil register as Frida Krubstein—a detail of no importance to a man who was in love; she came from Saxony and had been a servant at an inn. Then he disinherited his son, as far as he could.

And now that she is a respectable and respected widow, Madame de Loubancourt is received everywhere by society in those places of winter resort where people's bygone history is so rarely investigated; and when women bear a name, are pretty, and can waltz—as the Germans can—they are always well received.

The Upstart

DUPONTEL, you know, good-natured and stout, the type of a happy man, his fat cheeks red as ripe apples, his small, sandy mustache curling up over his thick lips, his prominent eyes that show no emotion or sorrow, and remind one of the calm eyes of a cow, or an ox, and his long body fixed on two little crooked legs, which gained him the nickname of "corkscrew" from some fairy of the opera ballet.

Dupontel, who had taken the trouble to be born, but not like the grand seigneurs whom Beaumarchais made fun of once upon a time, was ballasted with a respectable number of millions, as is becoming in the sole heir of a house that had sold household utensils and appliances for over a century.

Naturally, like every other *nouveau riche* who respects himself, he wished to appear something, to play at being a clubman, and also to play to the gallery, because he had been educated at Vaugirard and knew a little English; because he had gone through his service in the army for twelve months at Rouen; because he was a tolerable singer, could drive four-in-hand, and play lawn tennis.

Always studiedly well-dressed, too correct in every way, copying his way of speaking, his hats and his trousers from the three or four snobs who set the fashion, reproducing other people's witticisms, learning anecdotes and jokes by heart, like a lesson, to use them again at small parties, and constantly laughing, without knowing why his friends burst into roars of merriment. Of course, he was a perfect fool, but, after all, a capital fellow, to whom it was only right to extend a good deal of indulgence.

When he had had a great many love affairs and had made the discovery that in love money does not create happiness two thirds of the time, that they had all deceived him and made him perfectly ridiculous at the end of the week, Charles Dupontel made up his mind to settle down as a respectable married man, and to marry not from calculation or from reason, but for love.

One autumn afternoon at Auteuil he noticed in front of the club stand, among the number of pretty women who were standing round the braziers, a girl with such a lovely delicate complexion that it looked like apple blossoms; her hair was like threads of gold, and she was so slight and supple that she reminded him of those outlines of saints which one sees in old stained glass in church windows. There was also something enigmatical about her, for she had at the same time the delightfully ingenuous look of a schoolgirl during the holidays, and also of some enlightened young lady who already knows the how and the why of everything, who is exuberant with youth and life, and who is eagerly waiting for the moment when marriage will at length allow her to say and to do everything that comes into her head, and to amuse herself to satiety.

Then she had such tiny feet that they could have been held in a woman's hand, a waist that could have been clasped by a bracelet, curling eyelashes which fluttered like the wings of a butterfly, an impudent and sensual nose, and a vague, mocking smile that puckered her lips, like the petals of a rose.

Her father was a member of the Jockey Club, who was generally cleaned out, as they call it, at the Grand Prix, but who yet held his own bravely and went right on, and who kept himself afloat by prodigies of coolness and skill. He belonged to a race which could prove that his ancestors had been at the court of Charlemagne, and not musicians or cooks, as some people declared.

Her youth and beauty, and her father's pedigree, dazzled Dupontel, upset his brain, and altogether turned his mind upside down, and, combined, they seemed to him to be a mirage of happiness.

He obtained an introduction to her father, at the end of a game of baccarat, invited him to shoot with him, and a month later, as if it were an affair to be hurried over, he asked for, and obtained, the hand of Mademoiselle Thérèse de Montsaigne, and felt as happy as a miner who has discovered a vein of precious metal.

The young woman did not require more than twenty-four hours to discover that her husband was nothing but a ridiculous puppet, and immediately set about to consider how she might best escape from her cage and befool the poor fellow, who loved her with all his heart.

And she deceived him without the least pity or the slightest scruple; she did it as if from instinctive hatred, as if it were a necessity for her not only to make him ridiculous, but also to forget that she was bound in honor to him.

She was cruel, as all women are when they do not love, delighted in doing audacious and absurd things, and in visiting everything, and in braving danger. She seemed like a young colt that is intoxicated with the sun, the air, and its liberty, and gallops wildly across the meadows, jumps hedges and ditches, kicks, and whinnies joyously, and rolls about in the long, sweet grass.

But Dupontel remained quite undisturbed; he had not the slightest suspicion, and was the first to laugh when anybody told him some good story of a husband who had been deceived, although his wife repelled him, quarreled with him, and constantly pretended to be out of sorts or tired out, in order to escape from him. She seemed to take a malicious pleasure in annoying him by her personal remarks, her disenchanting answers, and her apparent listlessness.

They saw a great deal of company, and he called himself Du Pontel now, and even had thoughts of buying a Papal title; he only read certain newspapers, kept up a regular correspondence with the Orléans princes, was thinking of starting a racing stable, and finished up by believing that he really was a fashionable man, and strutted about, and was puffed out with conceit, as he had probably never read La Fontaine's fable in which he tells the story of the ass that is laden with relics which people salute, and so takes their bows to himself.

Suddenly, however, anonymous letters disturbed his quietude and tore the veil unexpectedly from his eyes.

At first he would tear them up without reading them and shrug his shoulders disdainfully; but he received so many of them, and the writer seemed so determined to dot his *i's* and cross his *t's* and to make things clear to him, that the unhappy man began to grow disturbed, and to watch and look about him. He instituted minute inquiries, and arrived at the conclusion that he no longer had the right to make fun of other husbands, and that he was the perfect counterpart of Sganarelle.

Furious at having been duped, he set a whole private detective agency at work, continually acted a part, and one evening appeared unexpectedly with a commissary of police in the snug little bachelor's quarters which concealed his wife's escapades.

Thérèse, who was terribly frightened and at her wits' end at being thus surprised, and pale with shame and terror, hid herself behind the curtains, while her lover, an officer of dragoons, was very much vexed at being mixed up in such a pinchbeck scandal, and at being caught by these men who were so correctly dressed in frock coats. He frowned angrily, and had to restrain himself so as not to fling his partner in guilt out of window.

The police commissary, who was calmly looking at this little scene with the coolness of a connoisseur prepared to verify the fact that they were caught *in flagrante delictu,* in an ironical voice said to the husband who had claimed his services:

" I must ask for your name in full, Monsieur? "

" Charles Joseph Edward Dupontel," was the answer. And as the commissary was writing it down from his dictation he added suddenly: " Du Pontel in two words, if you please, Monsieur le Commissionaire! "

The Venus of Braniza

IN Braniza, some years ago, lived a noted Talmud student who was no less renowned for his beautiful wife than for his learning, wisdom, and fear of God. The Venus of Braniza deserved her name both on account of her remarkable beauty and also as the wife of a man who was deeply versed in the Talmud; for the wives of the Jewish philosophers are, as a rule, ugly, or even possess some bodily defect.

The Talmud explains this in the following manner. It is well known that marriages are made in heaven, and at the birth of a boy a divine voice calls out the name of his future wife, and *vice versa*. But just as a good father tries to get rid of his good wares to outsiders, and only uses the damaged stuff at home for his children, so God bestows those women whom other men would not care to have on the Talmudists.

Well, God made an exception in the case of our Talmudist, and had bestowed a Venus on him, perhaps only in order to confirm the rule by means of this exception, and to make it appear less hard. His wife was a woman who would have done honor to any king's throne, or to a pedestal in any sculpture gallery. Tall, and with a wonderful voluptuous figure, she carried a strikingly beautiful head, surmounted by thick, black plaits, on her proud shoulders, while two large, dark eyes languished and glowed beneath her long lashes, and her beautiful hands looked as if they were carved out of ivory.

This beautiful woman, who seemed to have been designed by nature to rule, to see slaves at her feet, to provide occupation for the painter's brush, the sculptor's chisel, and the poet's pen, lived the life of a rare and beautiful flower shut up in a hothouse, for she sat the whole day long wrapped up in her costly fur jacket and looked down dreamily into the street.

She had no children; her husband, the philosopher, studied and prayed and studied again from early morning until late at night; his mistress was the Veiled Beauty, as the Talmudists call the Kabbalah. She paid no attention to her house, for she was rich and everything went of its own accord like clockwork; nobody came to see her, and she never went out of the house; she sat and dreamed and brooded and—yawned.

One day when a terrible storm of thunder and lightning had spent its fury over the town and all windows had been opened in order to let the Messiah in, the Jewish Venus was sitting, as usual, in her comfortable easy-chair, shivering in spite of her fur jacket, and was thinking, when suddenly she fixed her glowing eyes on the man who was sitting before the Talmud, swaying his body backward and forward, and said suddenly:

"Just tell me, when will Messias, the Son of David, come?"

"He will come," the philosopher replied, "when all the Jews have become either altogether virtuous or altogether vicious, says the Talmud."

"Do you believe that all the Jews will ever become virtuous?" the Venus continued.

"How can I believe that?"

"Then Messias will come when all the Jews have become vicious?"

The philosopher shrugged his shoulders and lost himself again in the labyrinth of the Talmud, out of which, so it is said, only one man ever returned in his sound mind, and the beautiful woman at the window again looked dreamily out on the heavy rain, while her white fingers played unconsciously with the dark fur of her magnificent jacket.

One day the Jewish philosopher had gone to a neighboring town where an important question of ritual was to be decided. Thanks to his learning, the question was settled sooner than he had expected, and instead of returning the next morning, as he had intended, he came back the same evening with a friend who was no less learned than himself. He got out of the carriage at his friend's house and went home on foot, and was not a little surprised when he saw his windows brilliantly illuminated, and found an officer's servant comfortably smoking his pipe in front of his house.

"What are you doing here?" he asked, in a friendly manner but with some curiosity, nevertheless.

"I am watching, in case the husband of the beautiful Jewess should come home unexpectedly."

"Indeed? Well, mind and keep a good lookout."

Saying this, the philosopher pretended to go away, but went into the house through the garden entrance at the back. When he got into the first room he found a table laid for two which had evidently only been left a short time previously. His wife was sitting as usual at her bedroom window wrapped in her fur jacket, but her cheeks were suspiciously red, and her dark eyes had not their usual languishing look, but now rested on her husband with a gaze which expressed at the same time satisfaction and mockery. At that moment he kicked against an object on the floor which gave forth a strange sound. He picked it up and examined it in the light. It was a pair of spurs.

"Who has been here with you?" the Talmudist said.

The Jewish Venus shrugged her shoulders contemptuously, but did not reply.

"Shall I tell you? The captain of hussars has been with you."

"And why should he not have been here with me?" she said, smoothing the fur on her jacket with her white hand.

"Woman! are you out of your mind?"

"I am in full possession of my senses," she replied, and a knowing smile hovered round her red, voluptuous lips. "But must I not also do my part in order that Messias may come and redeem us poor Jews?"

The Carters' Inn

THE coachman had jumped from his box and was walking slowly by the side of his thin horses, waking them up every moment by a cut of the whip or a coarse oath. He pointed to the top of the hill, where the windows of a solitary house were shining like yellow lamps, although it was quite late, and said to me:

"One gets a good drop there, Monsieur, and well served, by George!"

And his eyes flashed in his thin, sunburned face, which was of a deep brickdust color, while he smacked his lips like a drunkard who remembers a bottle of good liquor that he has lately drunk, and straightened himself up at the recollection.

"Yes, and well served by a wench who will turn your head for you before you have tilted your elbow and drunk a glass!"

The moon was rising behind the mountain peaks covered with snow which looked almost like blood under its rays, and were crowned by dark brown clouds, which whirled and floated about, reminding the passenger of some terrible Medusa's head. The gloomy plains of Capsir, which were traversed by torrents, with extensive meadows in which undefined forms were moving about, fields of rye like huge golden tablecovers, and here and there wretched villages and broad sheets of water, into which the stars seemed to look in a melancholy manner, opened out to the view. Damp gusts of wind swept along the road, bringing a strong smell of hay, of resin, of unknown flowers; and erratic pieces of rock were scattered on the surface like huge spectral boundary stones.

The driver pulled his broad-brimmed felt hat over his eyes, twirled his large mustache, and said in an obsequious voice:

"Does Monsieur wish to stop here? This is the place!"

It was a wretched wayside inn, with a reddish slate roof that looked as if it were suffering from leprosy, and before the door there stood three wagons drawn by mules and loaded with huge logs which took up nearly the whole of the road. The animals, who were in the habit of halting there, were dozing, and their heavy loads exhaled the odor of a pillaged forest.

Inside the house three wagoners were sitting in front of the fire, which crackled loudly; one of them, an old man, while the other two were young. Bottles and glasses stood on a large round table beside them, and they were singing and laughing boisterously. A woman with large round hips, and with a lace cap pinned to her hair, in the Catalan fashion, who looked strong and bold and had a certain amount of gracefulness about her, with a pretty but untidy head, was urging them to undo the strings of their great leather purses, and replied to their somewhat indelicate jokes in a shrill voice, as she sat on the knee of the youngest and allowed him to kiss her without any signs of shame.

The coachman pushed open the door, like a man who knows that he is at home.

"Good evening, Glaizette, and everybody; there is room for two more, I suppose?"

The wagoners did not speak, but looked at us cunningly and angrily, like dogs whose food had been taken from them and who show their teeth, ready to bite, while the woman shrugged her shoulders and looked into their eyes like some female wild beast tamer. Then she asked us, with a strange smile:

"What am I to bring you?"

"Two glasses of cognac, and the best you have in the cupboard, Glaizette," the coachman replied, rolling a cigarette.

While she was uncorking the bottle I noticed how green her eyes were—it was a fascinating, tempting green, like that of the great green grasshopper—and also how small her hands were, which showed that she did not use them much; how white her teeth were, and how her voice, which was rather rough, though cooing, had a cruel, and at the same time a coaxing, sound. She was the typical hostess of a wayside inn of that description, not overscrupulous and with a store of secrets.

I was anxious to escape from her as soon as possible; no longer to see her pale green eyes, and her mouth that bestowed caresses from pure charity, no longer to feel the woman with her beautiful, white hands so near me, so I threw her a piece of gold, and made my escape without saying a word to her, without waiting for any change, and without even wishing her good night, for I felt the caress of her smile and the disdainfulness of her looks. . .

The carriage started off at a gallop to Formiguères, amid a furious jingling of bells. I could not sleep any more; I wanted to know where that woman came from, but I was ashamed to ask the driver and to show any interest in such a creature, and when he began to talk, as we were going up another hill, as if he had guessed my thoughts, he told me all he knew about Glaizette. I listened to him with the attention of a child to whom somebody is telling some wonderful fairy tale.

She came from Fontpédrouze, a muleteers' village, where the men spend their time in drinking and gambling at the inn, when they are not traveling on the high roads with their mules, while the women do all the field work, carry the heaviest loads on their back, and lead a life of toil and misery.

Her father kept an inn, the girl grew up very happy; she was courted before she was fifteen, and was so coquettish that she was certain to be almost always found in front of her looking-glass, smiling at her own beauty, arranging her hair, trying to make herself like a young lady on the *prado*. And now as none of the family knew how to save a penny but spent more than they earned, and were like cracked jugs, from which the water escapes drop by drop, they found themselves ruined one fine day. So on the "Feast of Our Lady of Succor," when people go on a pilgrimage to Font Romea, and the villages are consequently deserted, the innkeeper set fire to the house. The crime was discovered through Glaizette, who could not make up her mind to leave behind her the looking-glass with which her room was adorned, and so had carried it off under her petticoat.

The parents were sentenced to many years' imprisonment, and being set free to live as best she could, the girl became a servant, going from one place to another, inherited some property from an old farmer, whom she had caught, as if he were a thrush on a limed twig, and with the money she had built this inn on the new road which was being built across the Capsir.

"A regular bad one, Monsieur," the coachman said, in conclusion, "a vixen such as one does not see now in the worst garrison towns, and who would open the door to the whole confraternity, and not at all avaricious, but thoroughly honest."

I interrupted him in spite of myself, as if his words had pained me, while I thought of those pale green eyes, those magic eyes, eyes to be dreamed about, the color of grasshoppers, and I looked for them, and saw them in the darkness; they danced before me like phosphorescent lights, and I would have given the whole contents of my purse to that man, if he would only have been silent and urged his horses on to full speed, so that their mad gallop might carry me off quickly, quickly and far, and continually farther from that girl.

An Adventure

"COME! Come!" said Pierre Dufaille, shrugging his shoulders. "What do you mean by saying that there are no more adventures? Say that there are no more adventurous men, and you will be right! Yes, nobody ventures to trust to chance in these days, for as soon as there is any slight mystery, or a spice of danger, they draw back. If, however, a man is willing to go into an adventure and to run the risk of anything that may happen, he can still meet with adventures, and even I, who never look for them, met with one in my life, and a very startling one; let me tell you about it.

"I was staying in Florence, and was living very quietly, and all I indulged in, in the way of adventures, was to listen occasionally to the immoral proposals with which every stranger is beset at night on the Piazza de la Signoria by some worthy Pandarus or other, with a head like that of a venerable priest. These excellent fellows generally introduce you to their families, where debauchery is carried on in a very simple and almost patriarchal fashion, and where one does not run the slightest risk.

"One day as I was admiring Benvenuto Cellini's wonderful Perseus, in front of the Loggia dei Lanzi, I suddenly felt my sleeve pulled somewhat roughly, and on turning round I found myself face to face with a woman of about fifty, who said to me with a strong German accent: 'You are French, Monsieur, are you not?' 'Certainly, I am,' I replied. 'And would you like to go home with a very pretty woman?'

"'Most certainly I should,' I replied, with a laugh.

"Nothing could have been funnier than the looks and the serious air of the procuress, or than the strangeness of the proposal, made in broad daylight, and in very bad French, but it was even worse when she added: 'Do you know everything they do in Paris?'

"'What do you mean, my good woman?' I asked her, rather startled. 'What is done in Paris that is not done everywhere else?'

"However, when she explained her meaning, I replied that I certainly could not, and as I was not quite so immodest as the lady, I blushed a little. But not for long, for almost immediately afterward I grew pale when she said:

"'I want to assure myself of it personally.' She said this in the same phlegmatic manner, which did not seem so funny to me now, but, on the contrary, rather frightened me.

"'What!' I said. 'Personally! You! Explain yourself!'

"If I had been rather surprised before, I was altogether astonished at her explanation. It was indeed an adventure, and was almost like a romance. I could scarcely believe my ears, but this is what she told me:

" She was the confidential attendant on a lady moving in high society, who wished to be initiated into the most secret refinements of Parisian high life, and who had done me the honor of choosing me for her companion. But then this preliminary test! 'By Jove!' I said to myself, 'this old German hag is not so stupid as she looks!' And I laughed in my sleeve as I listened to what she was saying to persuade me.

" 'My mistress is the prettiest woman you can dream of; a real beauty; springtime! A flower!'

" 'You must excuse me, but if your mistress is really like springtime and a flower, you (pray excuse me for being so blunt) are not exactly that, and perhaps I should not exactly be in a mood to humor you, my dear lady, in the same way that I might her.'

" She jumped back, astonished in turn: 'Why, I only want to satisfy myself with my own eyes; not by injuring you.' And she finished her explanation, which had been incomplete before. All she had to do was to go with me to Mother Patata's well-known establishment, and there to be present while I conversed with one of its fair and frail inhabitants.

" 'Oh!' I said to myself; 'I was mistaken in her tastes. She is, of course, an old, shriveled-up woman, as I guessed, but she is a specialist. This is interesting, upon my word! I never met with such a one before!'

" Here, gentlemen, I must beg you to allow me to

hide my face for a moment. What I said was evidently not strictly correct, and I am rather ashamed of it; my excuse must be that I was young, that Patata's was a celebrated place, of which I had heard wonderful things said, but the entry to which was barred me on account of my small means. Five napoleons was the price! Fancy! I could not treat myself to it, and so I accepted the good lady's offer. I do not say that it was not disagreeable, but what was I to do? And then, the old woman was a German, and so her five napoleons were a slight return for our five milliards, which we paid them as our war indemnity.

"Well, Patata's boarder was charming, the old woman was not too troublesome, and your humble servant did his best to sustain the ancient glory of Frenchmen.

"Let me drink my disgrace to the dregs! On the next day but one after I was waiting at the statue of Perseus. It was shameful, I confess, but I enjoyed the partial restitution of the five milliards, and it is surprising how a Frenchman loses his dignity when he is traveling.

"The good lady made her appearance at the appointed time. It was quite dark and I followed her without a word, for, after all, I was not very proud of the part I was playing. But if you only knew how fair that little girl at Patata's was! As I went along I thought only of her, and did not pay any attention to where we were going, and I was only roused from my reverie by hearing the old woman say: 'Here we are. Try to be as entertaining as you were the day before yesterday.'

"We were not outside Patata's house, but in a narrow street running by the side of a palace with high walls, and in front of us was a small door, which the old woman opened gently.

" For a moment I felt inclined to draw back. Apparently the old hag was also ardent on her own account! She had me in a trap! No doubt she wanted in her turn to make use of my small talents! But, no! That was impossible!

" ' Go in! Go in! ' she said. ' What are you afraid of? My mistress is so pretty, so pretty, much prettier than the little girl of the other day.'

" So it was really true, this story out of *The Arabian Nights?* Why not? And, after all, what was I risking? The good woman would certainly not injure me, and so I went in, though somewhat nervously.

" Oh! My friend, what an hour I spent then! Paradise! and it would be useless, impossible to describe it to you. Apartments fit for a princess, and one of those princesses out of fairy-tales, a fairy herself. An exquisite German woman, exquisite as German women can be when they try. An Undine of Heinrich Heine's, with hair like the Virgin Mary's, innocent blue eyes, and a skin like strawberries and cream.

" Suddenly, however, my Undine got up, and her face was convulsed with fury and pride. Then she rushed behind some hangings, where she began to give vent to a flood of German words, which I did not understand, while I remained standing, dumfounded. But just then the old woman came in, and said, shaking with fear: ' Quick, quick; dress yourself and go, if you do not wish to be killed! '

" I asked no question, for what was the use of trying to understand? Besides, the old woman, who grew more and more terrified, could not find any

French words, and chattered wildly. I jumped up and got into my shoes and overcoat, and ran down the stairs and in the street.

" Ten minutes later I recovered my breath and my senses, without knowing what streets I had been through, nor where I had come from, and I stole furtively into my hotel, as if I had been a malefactor.

" In the cafés the next morning nothing was talked of except a crime that had been committed during the night. A German baron had killed his wife with a revolver, but he had been liberated on bail, as he had appealed to his counsel, to whom he had given the following explanation, to the truth of which the lady companion of the Baroness had certified:

" She had been married to her husband almost by force, and detested him, and she had some particular reasons (which were not specified) for her hatred of him. In order to have her revenge on him she had had him seized, bound and gagged by four hired ruffians, who had been caught, and who had confessed everything. Thus reduced to immobility and unable to help himself, the Baron had been obliged to witness a degrading scene, where his wife caressed a Frenchman, thus outraging conjugal fidelity and German honor at the same time. As soon as he was set at liberty the Baron had punished his faithless wife, and was now seeking her accomplice."

" And what did you do? " some one asked Pierre Dufaille.

" The only thing I could do, by George! " he replied. " I put myself at the poor devil's disposal; it was his right, and so we fought a duel.

Alas! It was with swords, and he ran me right through the body. That was also his right, but he exceeded his right when he called me her *ponce*. Then I gave him his change, and as I fell I called out with all the strength that remained to me: 'A Frenchman! A Frenchman! Long live France!' "

The Man With the Blue Eyes

MONSIEUR PIERRE AGÉNOR DE VARGNES, the examining magistrate, the personification of dignity, sedateness, and correctness, was anything but a practical joker. Even in his wildest dreams he could never have perpetrated anything resembling a practical joke. It will thus be readily understood that a cold shiver passed through me when Monsieur Pierre Agénor de Vargnes did me the honor of sending a lady to call on me.

About eight o'clock one morning last winter, as he was leaving the house to go to the Palais de Justice, his footman handed him a card, on which was printed:

DOCTOR JAMES FERDINAND

Member of the Academy of Medicine
Port-au-Prince
Chevalier of the Legion of Honor

At the bottom of the card was written in pencil: "From Lady Frogère."

Monsieur de Vargnes knew the lady very well.

She was a very agreeable Creole from Hayti, whom he had met in many drawing-rooms; but, on the other hand, though the doctor's name did not awaken any recollections in him, his quality and titles alone required that he should grant him an interview, however short it might be. Therefore, although he was in a hurry to go out, Monsieur de Vargnes told the footman to show in his early visitor, but to tell him beforehand that his master was much pressed for time, as he had to go to the law courts.

When the doctor came in, in spite of his usual imperturbability, Monsieur de Vargnes could not restrain a movement of surprise, for the doctor presented that strange anomaly of being a negro of the purest, blackest type, with the eyes of a white man, of a man of the North, with pale, cold, clear, blue eyes; and his surprise increased when, after a few words of excuse for his untimely visit, he added, with an enigmatical smile:

"My eyes surprise you, do they not? I was sure that they would, and, to tell you the truth, I came here in order that you might look at them well, and never forget them."

His smile, and his words even more than his smile, seemed to be those of a madman. He spoke very softly, with that childish, lisping tone which is peculiar to negroes, and his mysterious, almost menacing words, therefore, sounded all the more as if they were uttered at random by an insane man. But his looks, the looks of those pale, cold, clear, blue eyes, were certainly not those of a madman. They clearly expressed menace, yes, menace, as well as irony, and, above all, implacable ferocity, and their glance was like a gleam of lightning which one could never forget.

"I have seen," Monsieur de Vargnes used to say when speaking about it, "the looks of many murderers, but in none of them have I ever observed such a depth of crime and of impudent security in crime."

And this impression was so strong that Monsieur de Vargnes thought that he was the victim of some hallucination, especially as when he spoke about his eyes, the doctor continued with a smile, and in his most childish accents: "Of course, Monsieur, you cannot understand what I am saying to you, and I must beg your pardon. To-morrow you will receive a letter which will explain it all to you, but, first of all, it was necessary that I should let you have a good, careful look at my eyes, my eyes, which are myself, my only and true self, as you will see."

With these words and with a polite bow, the doctor went out, leaving Monsieur de Vargnes extremely surprised, and a prey to doubt, as he said to himself:

"Is he merely a madman? His fierce expression and the criminal depth of his looks are perhaps caused merely by the extraordinary contrast between his fierce looks and his pale eyes."

And, absorbed in these thoughts, Monsieur de Vargnes unfortunately allowed several minutes to elapse, and then he thought to himself suddenly:

"No, I am not the sport of any hallucination, and this is no case of optical delusion. This man is evidently some terrible criminal, and I have altogether failed in my duty in not arresting him myself at once, though illegally, even at the risk of my life."

The judge ran downstairs in pursuit of the doctor, but it was too late; he had disappeared. In the afternoon he called on Madame Frogère to ask her whether she could tell him anything about the matter. She, however, had no acquaintance with the negro doctor, and was even able to assure the judge that he bore a fictitious title; for, as she was well acquainted with the upper classes in Hayti, she knew that the Academy of Medicine at Port-au-Prince had no doctor of that name among its members. As Monsieur de Vargnes persisted and gave a description of the doctor, especially mentioning his extraordinary eyes, Madame Frogère began to laugh, and said:

"You have certainly had to do with a practical joker, my dear Monsieur. The eyes which you have described are certainly those of a white man, and the individual must have been painted black."

On thinking it over Monsieur de Vargnes remembered that the doctor had nothing of the negro about him but his black skin, his woolly hair and beard, and his way of speaking, which could easily be affected, but nothing of the negro, not even the characteristic, undulating walk. Perhaps, after all, he was only a practical joker, and during the whole day Monsieur de Vargnes took refuge in that view, which rather wounded his dignity as a man of importance, but appeased his scruples as a magistrate.

The next day he received the promised letter, which was composed, as well as addressed, in type cut out of the newspapers. It was as follows:

"MONSIEUR: Doctor James Ferdinand does not exist, but the man whose eyes you saw does, and you will certainly recognize his eyes. This man has committed two crimes, for which he does not feel any remorse, but, as he is a psychologist, he is afraid of some day yielding to the irresistible temptation of confessing his crimes. You know better than any one (and that is your most powerful aid) with what imperious force criminals, especially intellectual ones, feel this temptation. That great poet, Edgar Poe, has written masterpieces on this subject, which express the truth exactly, but he has omitted to mention the last phenomenon, which I will tell you. Yes, I, a criminal, feel a terrible wish for somebody to know of my crimes, and when this desire is satisfied, and my secret has been revealed to a confidant, I shall be tranquil for the future, and be freed from this demon of perversity, which only tempts us once. Well! Now that is accomplished. You shall have my secret. From the day that you recognize me by my eyes, you will try and find out what I am guilty of, and how I was guilty, and you will discover it, being a master of your profession, which, by the by, has procured you the honor of having been chosen by me to bear the weight of this secret, which now is shared by us, and by us two alone. I say, advisedly, *by us two alone.* You could not, as a matter of fact, prove the reality of this secret to any one, unless I were to confess it, and I defy you to obtain my public confession, as I have confessed it to you, *and without danger to myself.*"

Three months later Monsieur de Vargnes met Monsieur X—— at an evening party, and at first sight, and without the slightest hesitation, he recognized in him those very pale, very cold, and very clear blue eyes, eyes which it was impossible to forget.

The man himself remained perfectly impassive, so that Monsieur de Vargnes was forced to say to himself:

"Probably I am the sport of a hallucination at this moment, or else there are two pairs of eyes in the world that are perfectly similar. And what eyes! Can it be possible?"

The magistrate instituted inquiries into the man's life, and he discovered something that removed all his doubts.

Five years previously Monsieur X—— had been a very poor but very brilliant medical student, who, although he never took his doctor's degree, had already made himself remarkable by his bacteriological researches.

A young and very rich widow had fallen in love with him and married him. She had one child by her first marriage, and in the space of six months, first the child and then the mother died of typhoid fever, and thus Monsieur X—— had inherited a large fortune, in due form, and without any possible dispute. Everybody said that he had attended to the two patients with the utmost devotion. Now, were these two deaths the two crimes mentioned in his letter?

But then Monsieur X—— must have poisoned his two victims with the microbes of typhoid fever, which he had skillfully cultivated so as to make the disease incurable, even with the most devoted care and attention. Why not?

"Do you believe it?" I asked Monsieur de Vargnes.

"Absolutely," he replied. "And the most terrible thing about it is that the villain is right when he defies me to force him to confess his crime publicly, for I see no means of obtaining a confession, none whatever. For a moment I thought of magnetism, but who could magnetize that man with those pale, cold, bright eyes? With such eyes he would force the magnetist to denounce himself as the culprit."

Then he said, with a deep sigh:

"Ah! Formerly there was something good about justice!"

And when he saw my inquiring looks he added:

"Formerly, justice had torture at its command."

"Upon my word," I replied, with all an author's unconscious and simple egotism, "it is quite certain that without the torture this strange tale will have no conclusion, and that is very unfortunate, as far as regards the story I intended to make out of it."

The Odalisque of Senichou

ABOUT twenty years ago, in Senichou, a suburb of Prague, lived a poor, honest couple who earned their bread by the sweat of their brows, the husband working in a large printing establishment, while his wife employed her spare time as a laundress. Their pride, and their only delight, was their daughter, Viteska, a vigorous, voluptuous-looking, handsome girl of eighteen, whom they brought up well and carefully. She worked for a dressmaker, and was thus able to help her parents a little, and she made use of her leisure moments in improving her education, and especially her music. She was a general favorite in the neighborhood, and was looked upon as a model by the whole suburb.

When she went to town to her work the tall girl, with her magnificent head like that of an ancient Bohemian Amazon, with its wealth of black hair, and her dark, sparkling yet soft eyes, attracted the looks of passers-by, in spite of her shabby dress, more than did the graceful, well-dressed ladies of the aristocracy. Frequently some young, wealthy idler would follow her home, and even try to get into conversation with her, but she always managed to get rid of them and their importunities, and did not require any escort, for she was quite capable of protecting herself from any insults.

One evening, however, on the suspension bridge, she met a man whose strange appearance made her glance at him with some interest, but perhaps with even more surprise. He was tall and handsome, with bright eyes and a black beard; he was very sunburned, and in his long coat, resembling a caftan, with a red fez on his head, he gave one the impression of an Oriental.

He had noticed her glance all the more as he himself had been so struck by her poor, and at the same time regal, appearance that he remained standing and looking at her as if he were devouring her with his eyes, so that Viteska, who was usually so fearless, cast down her eyes. She hurried on and he followed her, and the quicker she walked the more rapidly he followed, and at last, when they were in a narrow, dark street in the suburb, he suddenly said, in an insinuating voice: " May I offer you my arm, my pretty girl? "

" You can see that I am old enough to look after myself," Viteska replied hastily; " I am much obliged to you, and must beg you not to follow me any more; I am known in this neighborhood, and it might injure my reputation." " Oh, you are very much mistaken if you think you will get rid of me so easily," he replied. " I have just come from the East and am returning there soon. Come with me, and as I believe that you are as sensible as you are beautiful you will certainly make your fortune there, and I will warrant that before the end of a year you will be covered with diamonds, and be waited on by eunuchs and female slaves."

" I am a respectable girl, sir," she replied proudly, and tried to go ahead of him, but the stranger was immediately at her side again. " You were born to rule," he whispered to her. " Believe me, and I understand the matter, that you will live to be a sultana, if you have any luck."

The girl did not give him any answer, but walked on.

"But, at any rate, listen to me," the tempter continued.

" I will not listen to anything. Because I am poor you think it will be easy for you to tempt me," Viteska exclaimed; " but I am as virtuous as I am poor, and I should despise any position which I had to buy with my shame." They had reached the little house where her parents lived, and she ran in quickly and slammed the door behind her.

When she went into town the next morning the stranger was waiting at the corner of the street where she lived, and bowed to her very respectfully. "Allow me to speak a few words to you," he began. "I feel that I ought to beg your pardon for my behavior yesterday."

"Please let me go on my way quietly," the girl replied. "What will the neighbors think of me?"

"I did not know you," he went on, without paying any attention to her angry looks, "but your extraordinary beauty attracted me. Now that I know that you are as good as you are charming I wish very much to become better acquainted with you. Believe me, I have the most honorable intentions."

Unfortunately the bold stranger had taken the girl's fancy, and she could not find it in her heart to refuse him. "If you are really in earnest," she stammered, in charming confusion, "do not follow me about in the public streets, but come to my parents' house like a man of honor, and state your intentions there."

"I will certainly do so, and immediately, if you like," the stranger replied eagerly.

"No, no," Viteska said; "but come this evening, if you like."

The stranger bowed and left her, and really called on her parents the same evening. He introduced himself as Ireneus Krisapolis, a merchant of Smyrna, spoke of his brilliant circumstances, and finally declared that he loved Viteska passionately.

"That is all very well," the cautious father replied, "but what will it all lead to? Under no circumstances can I allow you to visit my daughter. Such a passion as yours often dies out as quickly as it rises, and a respectable girl is easily robbed of her virtue."

" And suppose I make up my mind to marry your daughter? " the stranger asked, after a moment's hesitation.

" Then I shall refer you to my child, for I shall never force Viteska to marry against her will," her father said.

The stranger seized the pretty girl's hand, and spoke in glowing terms of his love for her, of the luxury with which she would be surrounded in his house, of the wonders of the East, to which he hoped to take her, and at last Viteska consented to become his wife. Thereupon the stranger hurried on the arrangements for the wedding in a manner that made the most favorable impression on them all, and during the time before their marriage he lay at her feet like her humble slave.

As soon as they were married the newly married couple set off on their journey to Smyrna and promised to write as soon as they got there. But a month, then two and three, passed without the parents receiving a line from them, and as their anxiety increased every day the father, in terror, finally applied to the police.

The first thing was to write to the Consul at Smyrna for information. His reply was to the effect that no merchant of the name of Ireneus Krisapolis was known in Smyrna, and that he had never been there. The police, at the entreaties of the frantic parents, continued their investigations, but for a long time without any result. At last, however, they obtained a little light on the subject, but it was not at all satisfactory. The police at Pesth said that a man, whose personal appearance exactly agreed with the description of Viteska's husband, had a short time before carried off two girls from the Hungarian capital to Turkey, evidently intending to trade in that coveted, valuable commodity there, but that when he found that the authorities were on his track he had escaped from justice by a sudden flight.

* * * * * * *

Four years after Viteska's mysterious disappearance, two persons, a man and a woman, met in a narrow street in Damascus just as the Greek merchant had met Viteska on the suspension bridge at Prague. The man with the black beard, the red fez, and the long green caftan was no other than Ireneus Krisapolis. Matters appeared to be going well with him. He had his hands comfortably thrust into the red shawl which he wore round his waist, and a negro was walking behind him with a large parasol, while another carried his *chibuque.* A noble Turkish lady in a litter borne by four slaves met him; her face was covered with a white veil, all except a pair of large dark eyes that flashed threateningly at the merchant.

He smiled, for he thought that he had found favor in the eyes of an Eastern houri, and that flattered him; but soon he lost sight of her in the crowd, and forgot her almost immediately. The next morning, however, a eunuch of the Pasha's called on him, to his no small astonishment, and told him to come with him. He took him to the Sultan's most powerful deputy, who ruled as an absolute despot in Damascus. They went through dark narrow passages, and curtains were pushed aside which rustled as they closed behind him. At last they reached a large rotunda in the center of which was a beautiful fountain, and scarlet divans were placed all round it. Here the eunuch told the merchant to wait, and left him. He was puzzling his brains to know what the meaning of it all could be, when suddenly a tall, commanding woman came into the apartment. Again a pair of large, threatening eyes looked at him through the veil, and he knew from her green, gold-embroidered caftan that if it was not the Pasha's wife it was at least one of his favorites who was before him. He hurriedly knelt down, and, crossing his hands on his breast, put his forehead to the ground before her. But a clear, mocking laugh made him look up, and when the beautiful odalisque threw back her veil he uttered a cry of terror, for his wife, his deceived wife whom he had sold, was standing before him.

"Do you know me?" she asked, with quiet dignity.

"Viteska!"

"Yes, that was my name when I was your wife," she replied quickly, in a contemptuous voice; "but now that I am the Pasha's wife my name is Sarema. I do not suppose you ever expected to find me again, you wretch, when you sold me in Varna to an old Jewish profligate who was only half alive. You see I have got into better hands, and I have made my fortune, as you said I should do. Well? What do you expect of me; what thanks, what reward?"

The wretched man was lying, overwhelmed with confusion, at the feet of the woman whom he had so shamefully deceived, and could not find a word to say; he felt that he was lost, and had not even the courage to beg for mercy.

"You deserve death, you miscreant," Sarema continued. "You are in my hands and I can do whatever I please with you, for the Pasha has left your punishment to me alone. I ought to have you impaled, and to feast my eyes on your death agonies. That would be the smallest compensation for all the years of degradation that I have been through, and which I owe to you."

The wretched man cried, trembling all over and raising his hands to her in supplication: "Mercy, Viteska! Mercy!"

The odalisque's only reply was a laugh in which rang all the cruelty of an insulted woman's deceived heart. It seemed to give her pleasure to see the man whom she had loved and who had so shamefully trafficked in her beauty, in his abasement as he cringed before her, whining for his life as he clung to her knees; but at last she seemed to relent somewhat.

"I will give you your life, you miserable wretch," she said, "but you shall not go unpunished." So saying, she clapped her hands, and four black eunuchs came in and seized the favorite's unfortunate husband, and in a moment bound his hands and feet.

"I have changed my mind and he shall not be put to death," Sarema said, with a smile that made the traitor's blood run cold in his veins; "but give him a hundred blows with the bastinado, and I will stand by and count them."

"For God's sake," the merchant screamed, "I can never endure it."

"We will see about that," the favorite said coldly, "and if you die under it it is allotted you by fate; I am not going to retract my orders."

She threw herself down on the cushions and began to smoke a long pipe which a female slave handed to her on her knees. At a sign from her the eunuchs tied the wretched man's feet to the pole by which the soles of the culprit were raised, and began the terrible punishment. At the tenth blow the merchant began to roar like a wild animal, but his wife, whom he had betrayed, remained unmoved, carelessly blowing blue wreaths of smoke into the air, and, resting on her lovely arm, she watched his features, distorted by pain, with merciless enjoyment.

During the last blows he only groaned feebly, and then fainted.

* * * * * * *

A year later the dealer was caught with his female merchandise by the police in an Austrian town and handed over to justice, when he made a full confession, and by that means the parents of the Odalisque of Senichou heard of their daughter's position. As they knew that she was happy and surrounded by luxury, they made no attempt to get her out of the hands of the Pasha, who, like a thorough Mussulman, had become the slave of his slave.

The unfortunate husband was sent across the frontier when he was released from prison. His shameful traffic, however, flourishes still in spite of all the precautions of the police and of the consuls, and every year he provides the harems of the East with those voluptuous *Boxclanas,* especially from Bohemia and Hungary, who, in the eyes of a Mussulman, vie for the prize of beauty with the slender Circassian women.

The Accent

IT was a large house from whose white terraces overshadowed by vines one had a view of the sea. Tall pines formed a dome over the portico. There was a look of neglect and loneliness about the place, such as impresses one after a death or the departure of friends for other lands.

The interior wore a strange look, with unpacked boxes serving for wardrobes, and piles of bandboxes. There was an array of worm-eaten armchairs, into which bits of velvet and silk, cut from old dresses, had been twisted anyhow to make seats, and along the walls there were rows of rusty nails which made one think of old portraits and of pictures full of associations, which had one by one been bought for a low price by some second-hand furniture dealer.

The rooms were in disorder and furnished in a nondescript fashion, while velvets were hanging from the ceilings and in the corners, and seemed to show that as the servants were no longer paid except by hopes, they no longer did more than give them an accidental, careless touch with the broom occasionally. The drawing-room, which was extremely large, was full of useless knickknacks, rubbish which is put up for sale at stalls at watering-places, daubs—they could not be called paintings—of portraits and of flowers, and an old piano with yellow keys.

Such was the home where she who had been called the handsome Madame de Maurillac was spending her monotonous existence, like some unfortunate doll which inconstant, childish hands have thrown into a corner in a loft, she who almost passed for a professional beauty, and whose coquetries, at least so the faithful ones of the party said, had been able to excite a fleeting and last spark of desire in the dull eyes of the Emperor.

Like so many others, she and her husband had waited for his return from Elba, had discounted a fresh, immediate chance, had kept up boldly, and spent the remains of his fortune at that game of luxury.

On the day when the illusion vanished and he was forced to awake from his dream, Monsieur de Maurillac, without considering that he was leaving his wife and daughter behind him almost penniless, but not being able to make up his mind to come down in the world, to vegetate, to fight his creditors, to accept the alms of some sinecure, poisoned himself, like a shopgirl who is forsaken by her contemptuous sweetheart.

Madame de Maurillac did not mourn for him, and as this lamentable disaster made her interesting, and as she was assisted and supported by unexpected acts of kindness, and had a good adviser in one of those old Parisian lawyers who would get anybody out of the most inextricable difficulties, she managed to save something from the wreck, and to keep a small income. Then, reassured and emboldened, and resting her ultimate illusions and her chimerical hopes on her daughter's radiant beauty, and preparing for that last game in which they would risk everything, and, perhaps, also hoping that she might herself marry again, the ancient flirt arranged a double existence.

For months and months she disappeared from the world, and as a pretext for her isolation and for hiding herself in the country she alleged her daughter's delicate health, and also the important interests she had to look after in the South of France.

Her frivolous friends looked upon that as a great act of heroism, as something almost superhuman, and so courageous that incessant letters religiously kept her up in all the scandal and love adventures, in the falls as well as in the apotheoses of the capital.

The difficult struggle which Madame de Maurillac had to keep up in order to maintain her rank was really as fine as any of those campaigns in the twilight of glory, as those slow retreats where men only give way inch by inch and fight until the last cartridge is expended, until at last fresh troops arrive, reënforcements which bar the way to the enemy, and save the threatened flag.

Broken in by the same discipline and haunted by the same dream, mother and daughter lived on almost nothing in the dull, dilapidated house which the peasants called the château, and economized like poor people who have only a few hundred francs a year to live on. But Fabienne de Maurillac developed well in spite of everything, and grew up into a woman like some rare flower which is reared in a hot-house and preserved from the rough outside air.

In order that she might not lose her Parisian accent by speaking too much with the servants, who had remained peasants under their livery, Madame de Maurillac, who had not been able to bring a lady's maid with her, on account of the extra cost which her traveling expenses and wages would have entailed, and who, moreover, was afraid that some indiscretion might betray her maneuvers and cover her with ridicule, made up her mind to wait on her daughter herself. And Fabienne talked with nobody but her, saw nobody but her, and was like a little novice in a convent. Nobody was allowed to speak to her, or to interrupt her walks in the large garden, or on the white terraces that were reflected in the blue water.

As soon as the season for the country and the seaside came, however, they packed up their trunks and locked the doors of their house of exile. As they were not known, and by taking those terrible trains which stop at every station, and by which travelers arrive at their destination in the middle of the night, with the certainty that nobody will be waiting for you and see you get out of the carriage, they traveled third class, so that they might have a few banknotes the more with which to make a show.

A fortnight in Paris in the family house at Auteuil, a fortnight in which to try on dresses and bonnets and to show themselves, and then Trouville, Aix or Biarritz, the whole show complete, with parties succeeding parties; money was spent as if they did not know its value; balls at the casinos, constant flirtations, compromising intimacies, and the kind of admirers who immediately surround two pretty women, one in the radiant beauty of her eighteen years, and the other in the brightness of that maturity which beautiful September days bring with them.

Unfortunately, however, they had to do the same thing over again every year, and as if bad luck were continuing to follow them implacably, Madame de Maurillac and her daughter did not succeed in their endeavors, and did not manage during her usual absence from home to pick up some nice fellow who fell in love immediately, who took them seriously, and asked for Fabienne's hand; consequently, they were very unhappy. Their energies flagged, and their courage oozed away like water that escapes, drop by drop, through a crack in a jug. They grew low-spirited and no longer dared to be frank with each other and to exchange confidences and projects.

Fabienne, with her pale cheeks, her large eyes with blue circles round them, and her tight lips, looked like some captive princess who is tormented by constant ennui and troubled by evil suggestions, who dreams of flight and of escape from that prison where Fate holds her captive.

One night when the sky was covered with heavy thunderclouds and the heat was most oppressive, Madame de Maurillac called her daughter, whose room was next to hers. After calling her loudly for some time in vain, she sprang out of bed in terror and almost broke open the door with her trembling hands. The room was empty and the pillows untouched.

Almost distracted and foreseeing some irreparable misfortune, the poor woman ran all over the large house, and then rushed out into the garden, where the air was heavy with the scent of flowers. She had the appearance of some wild animal that is being pursued by a pack of hounds, tried to penetrate the darkness with her anxious looks, and gasped as if some one were holding her by the throat; but suddenly she staggered, uttered a painful cry, and fell down in a fit.

There, before her, in the shadow of the myrtle trees, Fabienne was sitting on the knees of a man—of the gardener—with both her arms round his neck and kissing him ardently, and as if to defy her mother and to show her how vain all her precautions and her vigilance had been, the girl was telling her lover, in the country dialect and in a cooing and delightful voice, how she adored him, and that she would be his. . . .

Madame de Maurillac is in a lunatic asylum, and Fabienne has married the gardener.

What could she have done better?

A Useful House

THROWING himself back in the great armchair, which he completely filled up, Royaumont, that picker-up of bits of pinchbeck, as they called him at the club, his fat sides shaking with laughter at the mere recollection of the funny story that he had promised to his friends, at last said:

"It is perfectly true Bordenave does not owe any one a penny and can go through any street he likes and publish those famous memoirs of sheriffs' officers which he has been writing for the last ten years, when he did not dare to go out, and in which he carefully brought out the characters and peculiarities of all those generous distributers of stamped paper with whom he had had dealings, their tricks and wiles, their weaknesses, their jokes, their manner of performing their duties, sometimes with brutal rudeness and at others with cunning good nature, now embarrassed and almost ashamed of their work, and again ironically jovial, as well as the artifices of their clerks to get a few crumbs from their employers' cake. The book will soon be published, and Machin, the vaudeville writer, has promised him a preface, so that it will be a most amusing work. You are surprised, eh? Confess that you are absolutely surprised, and I will lay you any bet you like that you will not guess how our excellent friend, whose existence is an inexplicable problem, has been able to settle with his creditors, and suddenly produce the requisite amount."

"Do get to the facts, confound it!" said Captain Hardeur, who was growing tired of all this verbiage.

"All right, I will get to them as quickly as possible," Royaumont replied, throwing the stump of his cigar into the fire. "I will clear my throat and begin. I suppose you all of you know that two better friends than Bordenave and Quillanet do not exist; neither of them could do without the other, and they have ended by dressing alike, by having the same gestures, the same laugh, the same walk, and the same inflections of voice, so that one would think that some close bond united them, and that they had been brought up together from childhood. There is, however, this great difference between them, that Royaumont is completely ruined and that all that he possesses are bundles of mortgages, ridiculous parchments which attest his ancient race, and chimerical hopes of inheriting money some day, though these expectations are already heavily hypothecated. Consequently, he is always on the lookout for some fresh expedients for raising money, though he is superbly indifferent about everything, while Sebastien Quillanet, of the banking house of Quillanet Brothers, must have an income of eight thousand francs a year, but is descended from an obscure laborer who managed to secure some of the national property, then he became an army contractor, speculated on defeat as well as victory, and Quillanet does not know now what to do with his money. But the millionaire is timid, dull, and always bored; the ruined spendthrift amuses him by his impertinent ways and his libertine jokes; he prompts him when he is at a loss for an answer, extricates him from his difficulties, serves as his guide in the great forests of Paris, which is strewn with so many pitfalls, and helps him to avoid those vulgar adventures which socially ruin a man, no matter how well ballasted he may be. Then Bordenave points out to him what women would make suitable companions for him, who make a man noted, and have the effect of some rare and beautiful flower in his buttonhole. He is the confidant of his intrigues, his guest when he gives small, special entertainments, his daily familiar table companion, and the buffoon whose sly humor one stimulates and whose worst witticisms one tolerates."

"Really, really," the Captain interrupted him, "you have been going on for more than a quarter of an hour without saying anything."

So Royaumont shrugged his shoulders and continued:

"Oh! you can be very annoying when you please, my dear fellow! . . . Last year, when Bordenave was at daggers drawn with his people, who were deafening him with their recriminations, were worrying him and threatening him with a lot of annoyance, Quillanet got married. A marriage of reason, which apparently changed his habits and his tastes, more especially as the banker was at that time associated with a perfect little marvel of a woman, a Parisian jewel of unspeakable attractions and of bewitching delicacy, that adorable Suzette Marly, who is just like a pocket Venus, and who in some prior stage of her existence must have been Phryne or Lesbia. Of course, he did not give up seeing her, but as he was bound to take some judicious precautions, which are necessary for a man who is deceiving his wife, he rented and furnished a house with a courtyard in front and a garden at the back, which one might think had been built to shelter some amorous folly. It was the nest that he had dreamed of, warm, snug, elegant, the walls covered with silk hangings of subdued tints, large pier-glasses, allegorical pictures, and filled with luxurious low furniture that seemed to invite flirtations. Bordenave occupied the ground floor, and the first floor served as a shrine for the banker and a luxurious abode for the beautiful Suzette. Well, just a week ago, in order to hide the situation better, Bordenave asked Quillanet and some other friends to one of those luncheons which he understands so well how to order, such a delicious luncheon, that before it was quite over every man and woman in this gay company were carrying on at a great rate, when the butler came in with an embarrassed look, and whispered something to him.

" 'Tell the gentleman that he has made a mistake, and ask him to leave me in peace,' Bordenave replied to him in an angry voice. The servant went out and returned immediately to say that the intruder was using threats, that he refused to leave the house, and even spoke of having recourse to the commissary of police. Bordenave frowned, threw his table napkin down, upset two glasses, and staggered out with a red face, swearing and stammering out:

" 'This is rather too much, and the fellow shall find out what going out of the window means, if he will not leave by the door.' But in the anteroom he found himself face to face with a very cool, polite, impassive gentleman, who said very quietly to him:

" 'You are Comte Robert de Bordenave, I believe, Monsieur?'

" 'Yes, Monsieur.'

" 'And the lease that you signed at the lawyer's, Monsieur Albin Calvert, in the Rue du Faubourg-Poissonnière, is in your name, I believe?'

" 'Certainly, Monsieur.'

" 'Then I regret extremely to have to tell you that if you are not in a position to pay the various accounts which different people have intrusted to me for collection here, I shall be obliged to seize all the furniture, pictures, plate, clothes, etc., which are here, in the presence of two witnesses who are waiting for me downstairs in the street.'

" 'I suppose this is some joke, Monsieur?'

" 'It would be a very poor joke, Monsieur le Comte, and one which I should certainly not allow myself toward you!'

" The situation was absolutely critical and ridiculous, the more so that in the dining-room the women, who were slightly the worse for wine, were tapping the wine glasses with their spoons and calling for him. What could he do except to explain his misadventure to Quillanet, who became sobered immediately, and rather than see his shrine violated, his secret disclosed, and his pictures, ornaments, and furniture sold, gave a check in due form for the claim there and then, though with a very wry face. And in spite of this, some people will deny that men who are utterly broke often have a stroke of luck!"

A Rupture

IT is just as I tell you, my dear fellow, those two poor things whom we all of us envied, who looked like a couple of pigeons when they were billing and cooing, and were always spooning until they made themselves ridiculous, now hate each other just as much as they used to adore each other. It is a complete break, and one of those which cannot be mended as you can mend an old plate! And all for a bit of nonsense, for something so funny that it ought to have brought them closer together and have made them laugh over it until they were ill. But how can a man explain himself when he is dying of jealousy, and when he keeps repeating to his terrified mistress: 'You are lying! you are lying!' When he shakes her, interrupts her while she is speaking, and says such hard things to her that at last she flies into a rage, has enough of it, becomes hard and mad, and thinks of nothing but of giving tit for tat and of paying him back in his own coin; does not care a straw about destroying his happiness, sends everything to the devil, and talks a lot of bosh, which she certainly does not believe. And then, because there is nothing so stupid and so obstinate in the whole world as lovers, neither he nor she will take the first step and own to having been in the wrong, and regret having gone too far; but both wait and watch and do not even write a few lines about nothing, which would restore peace. No, they let day succeed day, and there are feverish and sleepless nights when the bed seems so hard, so cheerless and so large, and habits get weakened, and the fire of love that was still smoldering at the bottom of the heart evaporates in smoke. By degrees both find some reason for what they wished to do, they think themselves idiots to lose time which will never return, in that fashion, and so good-by, and there you are! That is how Josine Cadenette and that great idiot Servance separated."

Lalie Spring had lighted a cigarette, and the blue smoke played about her fine, fair hair, which made one think of those last rays of the setting sun which pierce through the clouds at sunset. Resting her elbows on her knees, and with her chin in her hand in a dreamy attitude, she murmured:

"Sad, isn't it?"

"Bah!" I replied, "at their age people easily console themselves, and everything begins over again, even love!"

"Well, Josine has already found somebody else . . ."

"And did she tell you her story?"

"Of course she did, and it is such a joke! You must know that Servance is one of those fellows one would wish to have when one has time to amuse one's self, and so self-possessed that he would be capable of ruining all the seniors in a girls' school, and given to trifling as much as most men, so that Josine calls him 'perpetual motion.' He would have liked to go on with his fun until the day of judgment, and seemed to fancy that beds were not made to sleep in at all; but she could not get used to being deprived of nearly all her rest, and it really made her ill. But as she wished to be as conciliatory as possible, and to love and to be loved as ardently as in the past, and also to sleep off the effects of her happiness peacefully, she rented a small room in a distant quarter, in a quiet, shady street, giving out that she had just come from the country, and put hardly any furniture into it except a good bed and a dressing-table. Then she invented an old aunt for the occasion, who was ill and always grumbling, and who suffered from heart disease and lived in one of the suburbs; and so several times a week Josine took refuge in her sleeping place, and used to sleep late there, as if it had been some delicious abode where one forgets the whole world. Sometimes they forgot to call her at the proper time; she got back late, tired, with red and swollen eyelids, involved herself in lies, contradicted herself, and looked so much as if she had just come from the confessional, feeling horribly ashamed of herself, or as if she had hurried home from some assignation, that at last Servance worried himself about it, thought that he was being made a fool of, as so many of his comrades were, got into a rage, and made up his mind to set the matter straight, and to discover who this aunt of his mistress was who had so suddenly fallen from the skies.

"He was reduced to apply to an obliging agency, where they excited his jealousy, exasperated him day after day by making him believe that Josine Cadenette was making an absolute fool of him, had no more a sick aunt than she had any virtue, but that during the day she lived a fast life, and more than probably one of his own best friends was amusing himself at his expense.

"He was fool enough to believe these fellows, instead of going and watching Josine himself, putting his nose into the business, and going and knocking at the door of her room. He wanted to hear no more and would not listen to her. For a trifle, in spite of her tears, he would have turned the poor thing into the streets as if she had been a bundle of dirty linen. You may guess how she flew out at him and told him all sorts of things to annoy him; she let him believe he was not mistaken, that she had had enough of his affection, and that she was madly in love with another man. He grew very pale when she said that, looked at her furiously, clinched his teeth, and said in a hoarse voice:

"'Tell me his name, tell me his name!'

"'Oh!' she said teasingly, 'you know him very well!' and if I had not happened to have gone in I think there would have been a tragedy. . . . How stupid they are, and they were so happy and loved each other so! . . . And now Josie is living with fat Schweinssohn, a low scoundrel who will live upon her, and Servance has taken up with Sophie Labisque, who might easily be his mother; you know her, that bundle of red and yellow, who has been at that kind of thing for eighteen years, and whom Laglandée has christened *Sæcula sæculorum!*"

"By Jove! I should rather think I did!"

Virtue In the Ballet

WHEN the theatrical annalist discovers a true, honest heart behind the glamor of the stage he experiences a sensation of real pleasure. Of all the witches and semi-witches of that eternal Walpurgis night that represents the world, the ladies of the ballet have at all times and in all places been regarded as least like saints, although Hackländer repeatedly tried in his earlier novels to convince us that true virtue appears in tights and short petticoats, and is only to be found in ballet girls. Popular opinion does not bear out this theory, although here and there one finds a pearl in the dust and even in the dirt, as the following story will show:

Whenever a new, youthful dancer appeared at the Vienna Opera House the *habitués* began to go after her, and did not rest until the fresh young rose had been plucked by some hand or other. For how could those young and pretty, sometimes even beautiful, girls, who, with every right to life, love, and pleasure, were poor and had to subsist on a very small salary, resist the seduction of the smell of flowers and of the flash of diamonds? And if one resisted it, it was love, some real, strong passion, that gave her the strength to do so. But if she was then deserted she became only the more selfish and shameless.

At the beginning of the winter season of 185— the news was spread among the theatergoers that a girl of dazzling beauty was to appear in the ballet at the Court Theater. No one had yet seen that much-discussed phenomenon, but report spread her name from mouth to mouth; it was Satanella. The moment the bevy of supple figures in fluttering petticoats sprang on the stage every opera glass in the boxes and stalls was directed toward them, and at the same instant the new dancer was discovered, although she timidly kept in the background.

She was one of those girls who have the imprint of purity but at the same time present a splendid type of womanhood. She had the voluptuous form of Rubens' second wife, whom they called, not inappropriately, a Greek Helen, and her head with its delicate nose, its small full mouth, and its dark inquiring eyes, reminded people of the celebrated picture of the Flemish Venus in the Belvedere in Vienna.

She took the old guard of the Vienna Court Theater by storm, and the very next morning a perfect shower of *billets-doux,* jewels, and bouquets fell into the poor ballet girl's attic. For a moment she was dazzled by all this splendor, and looked at the gold bracelets, the brooches set with rubies and emeralds, and at the sparkling earrings, with flushed cheeks. But then an unspeakable terror of being lost and of sinking into degradation seized her, and she pushed the jewels away and was about to send them back. But, as is usual in such cases, her mother intervened in favor of "the generous gentlemen," and so the jewels were accepted, though the notes which accompanied them were not answered at present. A second and a third discharge of Cupid's artillery followed, without making any impression on the girl; a great number of her admirers fell off consequently, though some continued to send her presents and to assail her with love letters, and one had the courage to go still further.

He was a wealthy banker who called on the mother of Henrietta, the fair-haired ballet girl, and then one evening, quite unexpectedly, on the girl herself. He by no means met with the reception which he had expected from the pretty girl in a faded cotton gown. Henrietta treated him with a certain amount of good-humored respect, which had a much more unpleasant effect on him than that coldness and prudery which is so often synonymous with the coquetry and selfish speculation of a certain class of women. In spite of everything, however, he soon went to see her daily, and lavished his wealth on the beautiful dancer, although she asked for nothing, and he gave her no chance to refuse. The mother took pretty, small apartments for her daughter and herself in the Kärntnerstrasse and furnished them elegantly, hired a cook and housemaid, made an arrangement with a cabman, and clothed her daughter in silk, velvet, and valuable lace.

Henrietta said nothing except once when she remarked to her mother, in the presence of her admirer:

"Have you won a prize in the lottery?"

"Of course I have," her mother replied, with a laugh.

The girl, however, had given her heart elsewhere, and quite contrary to all precedent, to a man whose very name she was ignorant of, and who sent her no diamonds, and not even any flowers. But he was young and good-looking, and stood so retiringly, and so evidently in love, at the small side door of the Opera House every night, when she got out of her antediluvian rickety cab, and also when she got into it again after the performance, that she could not help noticing him. Soon he began to follow her wherever she went, and once he summoned up courage to speak to her when she had been to see a friend in a remote suburb. He was very nervous, but all that he said seemed very clear and logical, and she did not hesitate for a moment to confess that she returned his love.

"You have made me the happiest, and at the same time the most wretched, of men," he said, after a pause.

"What do you mean?" she said innocently.

"Do you not belong to another man?" he asked her in a sad voice.

She shook her abundant light curls.

"Up till now I have belonged to myself alone and I will prove it to you by requesting you to call upon me frequently and without restraint. Every one shall know that we are lovers. I am not ashamed of loving an honorable man, but I will not sell myself."

" But your splendid apartments and your dresses," her lover interposed shyly, " you cannot pay for them out of your salary."

" My mother has won a large prize in the lottery or made a hit on the Stock Exchange." And with these words the determined girl cut short all further explanations.

That same evening the young man paid his first visit, to the horror of the girl's mother, who was so interested in stocks, and he came again the next day, and nearly every day. Her mother's reproaches were of no more avail than the furious looks of the stockbroker, and when the latter one day asked for an explanation as to certain visits, the girl said proudly:

" That is very soon explained. He loves me and I love him, and I have promised to marry him."

He certainly did understand the explanation and disappeared, and with him the shower of gold ceased.

The mother cried and the daughter laughed. " I never gave the worn-out old rake any hopes, and what does it matter to me what bargain you made with him? I always thought that you had been lucky on the Stock Exchange. Now, however, we must seriously consider about giving up our apartments, and make up our minds to live as we did before."

" Are you really capable of making such a sacrifice for me as to renounce luxury and to share my poverty? " her lover said.

" Certainly I am! Is not that a matter of course when one loves? " the ballet girl replied, in surprise.

" Then let me inform you, my dear Henrietta,"

he said, "that I am not so poor as you think. I only wished to find out whether I could make myself loved for my own sake; I have done so. I am Count L——, and though I am a minor and dependent on my parents, yet I have enough to be able to retain your pretty rooms for you, and to offer you if not a luxurious, at any rate a comfortable, existence."

On hearing this, mama dried her tears immediately. Count L—— became the girl's acknowledged lover, and they passed the happiest hours together. Unselfish as the girl was, she was yet such a thoroughly ingenuous Viennese that whenever she saw anything that took her fancy, whether it was a dress, a cloak, or one of those pretty little ornaments for a side table, she used to express her admiration in such terms that Count L—— felt obliged to make her a present of the object in question. In this way he incurred enormous debts, which his father paid. At last, however, he inquired into the cause of all this extravagance, and when he discovered it, he gave his son the choice of giving up the dancer or of relinquishing all claims on the paternal fortune.

It was a sorrowful evening when Count L—— told Henrietta of his father's determination.

"If I do not give you up I shall be able to do nothing for you," he said at last, "and I do not even know how I should manage to live myself, for my father is just the man to allow me to want, if I defy him. That, however, is a very secondary consideration; but as a man of honor I cannot bind you, who have every right to luxury and enjoyment, and so I must set you at liberty from the moment that I cannot provide for you."

"But I will not give you up," Henrietta said proudly.

The young Count shook his head sadly.

"Do you love me?" the ballet girl said quickly.

"More than my life."

"Then we will not separate as long as I have anything," she continued.

And she would not give him up, and when his father actually turned Count L—— into the street she provided a home for both of them. He obtained a situation as a copyist clerk in a lawyer's office, and she sold her valuable dresses and jewels, and thus they lived for more than a year.

The young man's father did not appear to trouble his head about them, but nevertheless he knew everything that went on in their small home, and knew every article that the ballet girl sold; until at last, softened by such love and strength of character, he himself made the first advances to a reconciliation with his son.

And now Henrietta wears the diamonds which formerly belonged to the old Countess, and it is long since she was a ballet girl. She now sits by the side of her husband in a carriage bearing their coat-of-arms.

The Two Babylons QTY
Alexander Hislop
You may be surprised to learn that many traditions of Roman Catholicism in fact don't come from Christ's teachings but from an ancient Babylonian "Mystery" religion that was centered on Nimrod, his wife Semiramis, and a child Tammuz. This book shows how this ancient religion transformed itself as it incorporated Christ into its teachings....
Religion/History Pages:358
ISBN: *1-59462-010-5* *MSRP* ***$22.95***

The Power Of Concentration
Theron Q. Dumont
It is of the utmost value to learn how to concentrate. To make the greatest success of anything you must be able to concentrate your entire thought upon the idea you are working on. The person that is able to concentrate utilizes all constructive thoughts and shuts out all destructive ones...
Self Help/Inspirational Pages:196
ISBN: *1-59462-141-1* *MSRP* ***$14.95***

Rightly Dividing The Word
Clarence Larkin
The "Fundamental Doctrines" of the Christian Faith are clearly outlined in numerous books on Theology, but they are not available to the average reader and were mainly written for students. The Author has made it the work of his ministry to preach the "Fundamental Doctrines." To this end he has aimed to express them in the simplest and clearest manner..
Religion Pages:352
ISBN: *1-59462-334-1* *MSRP* ***$23.45***

The Law of Psychic Phenomena
Thomson Jay Hudson
"I do not expect this book to stand upon its literary merits; for if it is unsound in principle, felicity of diction cannot save it, and if sound, homeliness of expression cannot destroy it. My primary object in offering it to the public is to assist in bringing Psychology within the domain of the exact sciences. That this has never been accomplished..."
New Age Pages:420
ISBN: *1-59462-124-1* *MSRP* ***$29.95***

Beautiful Joe
Marshall Saunders
When Marshall visited the Moore family in 1892, she discovered Joe, a dog they had nursed back to health from his previous abusive home to live a happy life. So moved was she, that she wrote this classic masterpiece which won accolades and was recognized as a heartwarming symbol for humane animal treatment...
Fiction Pages:256
ISBN: *1-59462-261-2* *MSRP* ***$18.45***

The Codes Of Hammurabi And Moses - W. W. Davies
The discovery of the Hammurabi Code is one of the greatest achievements of archaeology, and is of paramount interest, not only to the student of the Bible, but also to all those interested in ancient history...
Religion Pages:132
ISBN: *1-59462-338-4* *MSRP* ***$12.95***

The Thirty-Six Dramatic Situations
Georges Polti
An incredibly useful guide for aspiring authors and playwrights. This volume categorizes every dramatic situation which could occur in a story and describes them in a list of 36 situations. A great aid to help inspire or formalize the creative writing process...
Self Help/Reference Pages:204
ISBN: *1-59462-134-9* *MSRP* ***$15.95***

The Go-Getter QTY
Kyne B. Peter
The Go Getter is the story of William Peck.He was a war veteran and amputee who will not be refused what he wants. Peck not only fights to find employment but continually proves himself more than competent at the many difficult test that are throw his way in the course of his early days with the Ricks Lumber Company...
Business/Self Help/Inspirational Pages:68
ISBN: *1-59462-186-1* *MSRP* ***$8.95***

Self Mastery
Emile Coue
Emile Coue came up with novel way to improve the lives of people. He was a pharmacist by trade and often saw ailing people. This lead him to develop autosuggestion, a form of self-hypnosis. At the time his theories weren't popular but over the years evidence is mounting that he was indeed right all along...
New Age/Self Help Pages:98
ISBN: *1-59462-189-6* *MSRP* ***$7.95***

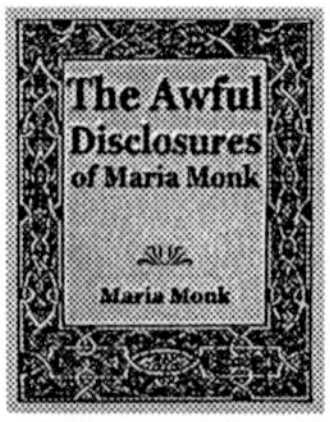

The Awful Disclosures Of
Maria Monk
"I cannot banish the scenes and characters of this book from my memory. To me it can never appear like an amusing fable, or lose its interest and importance. The story is one which is continually before me, and must return fresh to my mind with painful emotions as long as I live..."
Religion Pages:232
ISBN: *1-59462-160-8* *MSRP* ***$17.95***

As a Man Thinketh
James Allen
"This little volume (the result of meditation and experience) is not intended as an exhaustive treatise on the much-written-upon subject of the power of thought. It is suggestive rather than explanatory, its object being to stimulate men and women to the discovery and perception of the truth that by virtue of the thoughts which they choose and encourage..."
Inspirational/Self Help Pages:80
ISBN: *1-59462-231-0* *MSRP* ***$9.45***

The Enchanted April
Elizabeth Von Arnim
It began in a woman's club in London on a February afternoon, an uncomfortable club, and a miserable afternoon when Mrs. Wilkins, who had come down from Hampstead to shop and had lunched at her club, took up The Times from the table in the smoking-room...
Fiction Pages:368
ISBN: *1-59462-150-0* *MSRP* ***$23.45***

Holland - The History Of Netherlands
Thomas Colley Grattan
Thomas Grattan was a prestigious writer from Dublin who served as British Consul to the US. Among his works is an authoritative look at the history of Holland. A colorful and interesting look at history....
History/Politics Pages:408
ISBN: *1-59462-137-3* *MSRP* ***$26.95***

A Concise Dictionary of Middle English
A. L. Mayhew
Walter W. Skeat
The present work is intended to meet, in some measure, the requirements of those who wish to make some study of Middle-English, and who find a difficulty in obtaining such assistance as will enable them to find out the meanings and etymologies of the words most essential to their purpose...
Reference/History Pages:332
ISBN: *1-59462-119-5* *MSRP* ***$29.95***

The Witch-Cult in Western Europe QTY
Margaret Murray

The mass of existing material on this subject is so great that I have not attempted to make a survey of the whole of European "Witchcraft" but have confined myself to an intensive study of the cult in Great Britain. In order, however, to obtain a clearer understanding of the ritual and beliefs I have had recourse to French and Flemish sources...

Occult Pages:308
ISBN: *1-59462-126-8* *MSRP* ***$22.45*** ☐

Philosophy Of Natural Therapeutics QTY
Henry Lindlahr

We invite the earnest cooperation in this great work of all those who have awakened to the necessity for more rational living and for radical reform in healing methods...

Health/Philosophy/Self Help Pages:552
ISBN: *1-59462-132-2* *MSRP* ***$34.95*** ☐

The Science Of Psychic Healing
Yogi Ramacharaka

This book is not a book of theories it deals with facts. Its author regards the best of theories as but working hypotheses to be used only until better ones present themselves. The "fact" is the principal thing the essential thing to uncover which the tool, theory, is used...

New Age/Health Pages:180
ISBN: *1-59462-140-3* *MSRP* ***$13.95*** ☐

A Message to Garcia
Elbert Hubbard

This literary trifle, A Message to Garcia, was written one evening after supper, in a single hour. It was on the Twenty-second of February, Eighteen Hundred Ninety-nine, Washington's Birthday, and we were just going to press with the March Philistine...

New Age/Fiction Pages:92
ISBN: *1-59462-144-6* *MSRP* ***$9.95*** ☐

Bible Myths
Thomas Doane

In pursuing the study of the Bible Myths, facts pertaining thereto, in a condensed form, seemed to be greatly needed, and nowhere to be found. Widely scattered through hundreds of ancient and modern volumes, most of the contents of this book may indeed be found; but any previous attempt to trace exclusively the myths and legends...

Religion/History Pages:644
ISBN: *1-59462-163-2* *MSRP* ***$38.95*** ☐

The Book of Jasher
Alcuinus Flaccus Albinus

The Book of Jasher is an historical religious volume that many consider as a missing holy book from the Old Testament. Particularly studied by the Church of Later Day Saints and historians, it covers the history of the world from creation until the period of Judges in Israel. It's authenticity is bolstered due to a reference to the Book of Jasher in the Bible in Joshua 10:13

Religion/History Pages:276
ISBN: *1-59462-197-7* *MSRP* ***$18.95*** ☐

Tertium Organum
P. D. Ouspensky

A truly mind expanding writing that combines science with mysticism with unprecedented elegance. He presents the world we live in as a multi dimensional world and time as a motion through this world. But this isn't a cold and purely analytical explanation but a masterful presentation filled with similes and analogies...

New Age Pages:356
ISBN: *1-59462-205-1* *MSRP* ***$23.95*** ☐

The Titan
Theodore Dreiser

"When Frank Algernon Cowperwood emerged from the Eastern District Penitentiary, in Philadelphia he realized that the old life he had lived in that city since boyhood was ended. His youth was gone, and with it had been lost the great business prospects of his earlier manhood. He must begin again..."

Fiction Pages:564
ISBN: *1-59462-220-5* *MSRP* ***$33.95*** ☐

Advance Course in Yogi Philosophy
Yogi Ramacharaka

"The twelve lessons forming this volume were originally issued in the shape of monthly lessons, known as "The Advanced Course in Yogi Philosophy and Oriental Occultism" during a period of twelve months beginning with October, 1904, and ending September, 1905."

Philosophy/Inspirational/Self Help Pages:340
ISBN: *1-59462-229-9* *MSRP* ***$22.95*** ☐

Biblical Essays
J. B. Lightfoot

About one-third of the present volume has already seen the light. The opening essay "On the Internal Evidence for the Authenticity and Genuineness of St John's Gospel" was published in the "Expositor" in the early months of 1890, and has been reprinted since...

Religion/History Pages:480
ISBN: *1-59462-238-8* *MSRP* ***$30.95*** ☐

Ambassador Morgenthau's Story
Henry Morgenthau

"By this time the American people have probably become convinced that the Germans deliberately planned the conquest of the world. Yet they hesitate to convict on circumstantial evidence and for this reason all eye witnesses to this, the greatest crime in modern history, should volunteer their testimony..."

History Pages:472
ISBN: *1-59462-244-2* *MSRP* ***$29.95*** ☐

The Settlement Cook Book
Simon Kander

A legacy from the civil war, this book is a classic "American charity cookbook," which was used for fundraisers starting in Milwaukee. While it has transformed over the years, this printing provides great recipes from American history. Over two million copies have been sold. This volume contains a rich collection of recipes from noted chefs and hostesses of the turn of the century...

How-to Pages:472
ISBN: *1-59462-256-6* *MSRP* ***$29.95*** ☐

The Aquarian Gospel of Jesus the Christ
Levi Dowling

A retelling of Jesus' story which tells us what happened during the twenty year gap left by the Bible's New Testament. It tells of his travels to the far-east where he studied with the masters and fought against the rigid caste system. This book has enjoyed a resurgence in modern America and provides spiritual insight with charm. Its influences can be seen throughout the Age of Aquarius.

Religion Pages:264
ISBN: *1-59462-321-X* *MSRP* ***$18.95*** ☐

My Life and Work
Henry Ford

Henry Ford revolutionized the world with his implementation of mass production for the Model T automobile. Gain valuable business insight into his life and work with his own auto-biography... "We have only started on our development of our country we have not as yet, with all our talk of wonderful progress, done more than scratch the surface. The progress has been wonderful enough but..."

Biographies/History/Business Pages:300
ISBN: *1-59462-198-5* *MSRP* ***$21.95*** ☐

www.bookjungle.com *email: sales@bookjungle.com fax: 630-214-0564 mail: Book Jungle PO Box 2226 Champaign, IL 61825*

QTY

The Rosicrucian Cosmo-Conception Mystic Christianity *by* ***Max Heindel*** **ISBN:** ***1-59462-188-8*** **$38.95**
The Rosicrucian Cosmo-conception is not dogmatic, neither does it appeal to any other authority than the reason of the student. It is: not controversial, but is: sent forth in the, hope that it may help to clear... *New Age Religion Pages 646*

Abandonment To Divine Providence *by* ***Jean-Pierre de Caussade*** **ISBN:** ***1-59462-228-0*** **$25.95**
"The Rev. Jean Pierre de Caussade was one of the most remarkable spiritual writers of the Society of Jesus in France in the 18th Century. His death took place at Toulouse in 1751. His works have gone through many editions and have been republished... *Inspirational/Religion Pages 400*

Mental Chemistry *by* ***Charles Haanel*** **ISBN:** ***1-59462-192-6*** **$23.95**
Mental Chemistry allows the change of material conditions by combining and appropriately utilizing the power of the mind. Much like applied chemistry creates something new and unique out of careful combinations of chemicals the mastery of mental chemistry... *New Age Pages 354*

The Letters of Robert Browning and Elizabeth Barret Barrett 1845-1846 vol II **ISBN:** ***1-59462-193-4*** **$35.95**
by ***Robert Browning*** *and* ***Elizabeth Barrett*** *Biographies Pages 596*

Gleanings In Genesis (volume I) *by* ***Arthur W. Pink*** **ISBN:** ***1-59462-130-6*** **$27.45**
Appropriately has Genesis been termed "the seed plot of the Bible" for in it we have, in germ form, almost all of the great doctrines which are afterwards fully developed in the books of Scripture which follow... *Religion/Inspirational Pages 420*

The Master Key *by* ***L. W. de Laurence*** **ISBN:** ***1-59462-001-6*** **$30.95**
In no branch of human knowledge has there been a more lively increase of the spirit of research during the past few years than in the study of Psychology, Concentration and Mental Discipline. The requests for authentic lessons in Thought Control, Mental Discipline and... *New Age/Business Pages 422*

The Lesser Key Of Solomon Goetia *by* ***L. W. de Laurence*** **ISBN:** ***1-59462-092-X*** **$9.95**
This translation of the first book of the "Lernegton" which is now for the first time made accessible to students of Talismanic Magic was done, after careful collation and edition, from numerous Ancient Manuscripts in Hebrew, Latin, and French... *New Age/Occult Pages 92*

Rubaiyat Of Omar Khayyam *by* ***Edward Fitzgerald*** **ISBN:***1-59462-332-5* **$13.95**
Edward Fitzgerald, whom the world has already learned, in spite of his own efforts to remain within the shadow of anonymity, to look upon as one of the rarest poets of the century, was born at Bredfield, in Suffolk, on the 31st of March, 1809. He was the third son of John Purcell... *Music Pages 172*

Ancient Law *by* ***Henry Maine*** **ISBN:** ***1-59462-128-4*** **$29.95**
The chief object of the following pages is to indicate some of the earliest ideas of mankind, as they are reflected in Ancient Law, and to point out the relation of those ideas to modern thought. *Religiom/History Pages 452*

Far-Away Stories *by* ***William J. Locke*** **ISBN:** ***1-59462-129-2*** **$19.45**
"Good wine needs no bush, but a collection of mixed vintages does. And this book is just such a collection. Some of the stories I do not want to remain buried for ever in the museum files of dead magazine-numbers an author's not unpardonable vanity..." *Fiction Pages 272*

Life of David Crockett *by* ***David Crockett*** **ISBN:** ***1-59462-250-7*** **$27.45**
"Colonel David Crockett was one of the most remarkable men of the times in which he lived. Born in humble life, but gifted with a strong will, an indomitable courage, and unremitting perseverance... *Biographies/New Age Pages 424*

Lip-Reading *by* ***Edward Nitchie*** **ISBN:** ***1-59462-206-X*** **$25.95**
Edward B. Nitchie, founder of the New York School for the Hard of Hearing, now the Nitchie School of Lip-Reading, Inc, wrote "LIP-READING Principles and Practice". The development and perfecting of this meritorious work on lip-reading was an undertaking... *How-to Pages 400*

A Handbook of Suggestive Therapeutics, Applied Hypnotism, Psychic Science **ISBN:** ***1-59462-214-0*** **$24.95**
by ***Henry Munro*** *Health/New Age/Health/Self-help Pages 376*

A Doll's House: and Two Other Plays *by* ***Henrik Ibsen*** **ISBN:** ***1-59462-112-8*** **$19.95**
Henrik Ibsen created this classic when in revolutionary 1848 Rome. Introducing some striking concepts in playwriting for the realist genre, this play has been studied the world over. *Fiction/Classics/Plays 308*

The Light of Asia *by* ***sir Edwin Arnold*** **ISBN:** ***1-59462-204-3*** **$13.95**
In this poetic masterpiece, Edwin Arnold describes the life and teachings of Buddha. The man who was to become known as Buddha to the world was born as Prince Gautama of India but he rejected the worldly riches and abandoned the reigns of power when... *Religion/History/Biographies Pages 170*

The Complete Works of Guy de Maupassant *by* ***Guy de Maupassant*** **ISBN:** ***1-59462-157-8*** **$16.95**
"For days and days, nights and nights, I had dreamed of that first kiss which was to consecrate our engagement, and I knew not on what spot I should put my lips..." *Fiction/Classics Pages 240*

The Art of Cross-Examination *by* ***Francis L. Wellman*** **ISBN:** ***1-59462-309-0*** **$26.95**
Written by a renowned trial lawyer, Wellman imparts his experience and uses case studies to explain how to use psychology to extract desired information through questioning. *How-to/Science/Reference Pages 408*

Answered or Unanswered? *by* ***Louisa Vaughan*** **ISBN:** ***1-59462-248-5*** **$10.95**
Miracles of Faith in China *Religion Pages 112*

The Edinburgh Lectures on Mental Science (1909) *by* ***Thomas*** **ISBN:** ***1-59462-008-3*** **$11.95**
This book contains the substance of a course of lectures recently given by the writer in the Queen Street Hall, Edinburgh. Its purpose is to indicate the Natural Principles governing the relation between Mental Action and Material Conditions... *New Age/Psychology Pages 148*

Ayesha *by* ***H. Rider Haggard*** **ISBN:** ***1-59462-301-5*** **$24.95**
Verily and indeed it is the unexpected that happens! Probably if there was one person upon the earth from whom the Editor of this, and of a certain previous history, did not expect to hear again... *Classics Pages 380*

Ayala's Angel *by* ***Anthony Trollope*** **ISBN:** ***1-59462-352-X*** **$29.95**
The two girls were both pretty, but Lucy who was twenty-one who supposed to be simple and comparatively unattractive, whereas Ayala was credited, as her Bombwhat romantic name might show, with poetic charm and a taste for romance. Ayala when her father died was nineteen... *Fiction Pages 484*

The American Commonwealth *by* ***James Bryce*** **ISBN:** ***1-59462-286-8*** **$34.45**
An interpretation of American democratic political theory. It examines political mechanics and society from the perspective of Scotsman James Bryce *Politics Pages 572*

Stories of the Pilgrims *by* ***Margaret P. Pumphrey*** **ISBN:** ***1-59462-116-0*** **$17.95**
This book explores pilgrims religious oppression in England as well as their escape to Holland and eventual crossing to America on the Mayflower, and their early days in New England... *History Pages 268*

Printed in the United States
82343LV00004B/14